Anonymous

St. Matthew and St. Mark and the general Epistles

Anonymous

St. Matthew and St. Mark and the general Epistles

ISBN/EAN: 9783337730871

Printed in Europe, USA, Canada, Australia, Japan

Cover: Foto ©ninafisch / pixelio.de

More available books at **www.hansebooks.com**

THE MODERN READER'S BIBLE

A SERIES OF WORKS FROM THE SACRED SCRIPTURES PRESENTED
IN MODERN LITERARY FORM

ST. MATTHEW AND ST. MARK

AND

THE GENERAL EPISTLES

EDITED, WITH AN INTRODUCTION AND NOTES

BY

RICHARD G. MOULTON, M.A. (CAMB.), PH.D. (PENN.)

PROFESSOR OF LITERATURE IN ENGLISH IN THE
UNIVERSITY OF CHICAGO

New York
THE MACMILLAN COMPANY

LONDON: MACMILLAN & CO., LTD.

1898

All rights reserved

COPYRIGHT, 1898,
By THE MACMILLAN COMPANY.

Set up and electrotyped January, 1898. Reprinted August, 1898.

Norwood Press
J. S. Cushing & Co. — Berwick & Smith
Norwood Mass. U.S.A.

INTRODUCTION

THE series of books which make up the New Testament group themselves into a clear and interesting unity.

> The Acts and Sayings of Jesus
> (Gospels)
>
> The Acts of the Apostles
> The Sayings of the Apostles (or Epistles)
>
> The Prophetic Vision of the New Testament

This last, by its revival of the form and matter of ancient prophecy in application to the Christian dispensation, makes a link binding together the Old Testament and the New. The gospels, moreover, are for their age a sacred history like the historic books of the Old Testament; and the epistles, like portions of *The Chronicles*, may be regarded as documents illustrative of the history. But such a description of them would obviously be inadequate. Indeed, it is extremely difficult to fit the gospels into any literary classification: from the point of view of literature, no less than of theology, they are a class of works that stand by themselves. They are our historic authorities for the most important of all events; yet the purpose of their authors is not to write history. Though they are concerned solely with the life of Jesus, yet they would be imperfectly described as biographies. They treasure up every saying of the Master, as certain books of the Old Testament collect the sayings of the wise; yet but small portions of the gospels have any resemblance to wisdom literature. It would be easier to associate them with the prophetic books of the Old Testament. But the prophets use every variety of literary form to emphasise and recommend the message from above of which they are interpreters; Jesus Christ is himself the authority of the message he brings, and those through whom we learn of him are anxious to record and not to interpret. Moreover, an examination into the literary form of the gospels would be inextricably interwoven with another kind of enquiry: the close resemblances between these books, and their not less interesting differences, necessarily raise the question of their mutual relations, of their authorship, and possible connection with a common original. Such questions as these cannot be discussed here: not only do they belong to the domain of history rather than literature, but they are, of all historical questions, the questions on which there has been the fiercest controversy, and the widest difference and fluctuation of opinion. The aim of the present series

Introduction

goes no further than the placing the New Testament before the reader in the form which will best enable him to read each book in the light that may be collected from itself.

In attempting thus to bring the New Testament works into the series of the Modern Reader's Bible, attention is attracted first by the *Gospel of St. Luke*. Not only does this more than the rest exhibit the character of ordinary history, but further it has a continuation in the *Acts of the Apostles*, carrying the history a generation later. I propose to include these in a single number of the series, the size of which will necessitate two volumes. Again, of the epistles, the larger number stand in the name of St. Paul, by far the most prominent of those engaged in extending the boundaries of the early church. It seems a convenient course to place these Pauline Epistles in the same number of the series as the history, each epistle inserted at the point of the narrative with which it appears to connect itself, though, of course, distinguished from the history by difference of type. Such arrangement will assimilate this number of the series to *The Exodus*, in which, by the plan of Old Testament writers, the constitutional documents are made to stand at those points of the historic narrative with which they are to be associated. In another important respect this double volume of *St. Luke and St. Paul* will be a counterpart of the earlier historic series: it will give the History of the New Testament Church as presented by itself. Again, without entering into disputed

→❧ Introduction

questions of authorship, it seems a natural arrangement to include in a single volume the writings attributed by long tradition to St. John. There remains the present volume — published by request out of its course — as a miscellany in which are contained the other works of the New Testament: the *Gospels of St. Matthew* and *St. Mark*, and *The General Epistles*.

It is a leading purpose of the present series to use all devices of printing and page setting in order to assist the reader to catch the literary form of what he reads. The gospels have the twofold purpose of presenting alike the Acts and the Sayings of Jesus; I have thought it worth while, in this edition, to discriminate to the eye these two elements of the gospel narrative. But of course every word spoken by Jesus is not a 'Saying' in this sense. It would manifestly be improper to put forward as a 'Saying' of Jesus his words to the Canaanitish woman, "I was not sent but unto the lost sheep of the house of Israel": such words make only a stage in an uncompleted incident. It is the independent Sayings that I have distinguished by difference of type. No one will be misled into understanding such Sayings as more sacred or precious than other words of Christ; the words spoken on the cross, and in the institution of the Lord's Supper, are among those not so distinguished. The difference intended to be conveyed is merely that the Sayings printed in heavy type can be studied as independent wholes: other words

Introduction

of Jesus are merged in the incidents of which they form a portion.

Apart from this, the chief work of arrangement in the present edition has consisted in the division of each book into its proper sections, and the supply of headings. I believe that there are few things which assist intelligent reading more than the mere mechanism of division and subdivision, provided such arrangement is based upon independent study of each of the works so treated; the plan followed in old versions of a uniform division of chapters and verses for all books of Scripture alike carries its condemnation upon the surface. The notes will be few: they attempt neither theological nor historical discussion, but merely offer assistance towards catching the connection and emphasis of the writer's thought. And the editor believes that no small number of his readers will welcome notes which make it their first aim to reduce the interruption of annotation to a minimum.

I

The Gospel of St. Matthew has two highly distinctive marks of individuality. One of these lies upon the surface. No one can read the book without perceiving that the author writes as a Hebrew to Hebrews; possibly he wrote originally in the Hebrew tongue. The Old Testament is continually before the eyes of Matthew as he composes the book with which the New Testament is to commence.

Introduction

Not only does he see in Jesus the fulfilment of Messianic prophecy, but the very phrases of the prophets come back to him with a new significance in the light of the story he is telling. The birth of Jesus from a virgin mother recalls Isaiah's sign of the virgin and her mystic son Immanuel. The words of yearning which Hosea puts into the mouth of God, *When Israel was a child I loved him and called my son out of Egypt*, are a reminiscence associated with the flight into Egypt and the return by warning in a dream from God. And Jeremiah's picture of Rachel weeping for her children, an item in his drama of Israel's restoration, is recalled to Matthew by the massacre of the innocents. There is again an idiosyncrasy of Hebrew style which in Matthew's gospel is found to have penetrated into the very scheme of his arrangement: the structure is continually based on the number seven. The collection of Christ's teaching which we call the Sermon on the Mount is arranged by Matthew in seven natural divisions; the seventh of these is a series of seven separate sayings, and the first section is a beatitude expanded into sevenfold illustration. Other evangelists speak of different expeditions of apostles sent out by Jesus, with brief instructions. Matthew gathers all these instructions together into a single sevenfold commission. All the writers make prominent the institution of the parable as a form of teaching: Matthew illustrates this section with exactly seven parables. The denunciations of Pharisaic hypocrisy are by

Introduction

Matthew gathered together at one point, and the discourse is so modelled as to recall the Sevenfold Woe of Isaiah. In the discourse on the end of all things the three evangelists follow so closely the same order of thought that the division of the paragraphs in all three correspond; but while Mark and Luke stop with the fifth of these paragraphs, Matthew adds parables and additional foreshowings until the number of divisions has reached seven. It must not be supposed that there is anything strange or artificial in this repetition of the sevenfold structure. I have pointed out in previous volumes how widely such arrangement prevails in the Old Testament. Most of the prophetic books lend themselves to a sevenfold arrangement; the great Isaiahan Rhapsody not only has seven main divisions, but the first of them contains a movement seven times repeated; the last discourse of *The Wisdom of Solomon* supports its theme with seven illustrations, one of which is broken by a sevenfold digression. All that is implied in such a feature of style is an extreme sense of orderly arrangement; and to the Hebrew mind order suggests the number seven.

The other distinguishing feature of St. Matthew is his philosophic grasp of the ministry of Jesus as a great historic movement. All the three evangelists use repeatedly the phrase 'the kingdom of heaven' or 'the kingdom of God,' which must have been a regular expression of Jesus himself. But Matthew is wholly occupied in tracing the

Introduction

development of this 'kingdom of heaven': its development as a conception, from the mere idea of a counterpart to Roman empire, which animated those who first hailed the Baptist's announcement, to the conception of a spiritual kingdom founded on service and self-denial, which Jesus with such difficulty inculcated in the minds of the inner circle of disciples; the development again of a visible kingdom of heaven in human society, in antagonism with the ruling powers which crushed it only to give it its power of finally rising. It is natural that an historian of this type should give special prominence to the discourses of Jesus; further, it is the practice of St. Matthew to gather together from different parts of the life of his Master details of teaching that have a mutual connection, and to mass these together in a single discourse at the point where they will be most effective. It is the same with regard to incident. Modern harmonists who curiously enquire into the exact succession of incidents in the life of Christ find *St. Matthew* the least historic of the gospels. But this is only because the mind of this writer is intent on the philosophic sequence, and a grouping of incidents that brings out their connection and significance. As we follow his narrative we catch a majestic movement of events that draws the whole life and ministry of Christ into a clear unity.

The Gospel of St. Matthew is in the present edition divided into what appear to be its twelve natural sections

Introduction

—I must not call them chapters, since that name has been appropriated by the traditional divisions. Of these the first two are preliminary, relating the Birth of Jesus, and his first appearance in public under the Ministry of John the Baptist. Here Matthew confines himself to the barest outline of narration, except in one respect: that in the first section more than anywhere else is found this writer's characteristic use of the Old Testament. There is a striking contrast between the narratives of Matthew and Luke at this point. The latter seems to have carefully collected all that was to be learned of the early life of Jesus, and he relates the incidents with special fulness. St. Matthew, on the other hand, seems guided in his very selection of incidents by the thoughts of prophetic literature which they call up.

The third section opens the ministry of Jesus with the extended discourse which venerable tradition has styled the Sermon on the Mount. Yet this is obviously no sermon in the modern sense. Internal evidence and comparison with the other gospels show that here, as elsewhere, Matthew is drawing together into one view characteristic examples of the teaching of Jesus; in the present case his earlier teaching is exemplified, and it is likely enough that an outward characteristic of the same period might be the discourse from a mountain slope. The teaching is the teaching of Jesus; the arrangement is that of St. Matthew. It is natural that a Hebrew philosopher should make the

Introduction

basis of his arrangement a literary form prominent in the Hebrew philosophy we call Wisdom literature. This is what I have termed the Maxim — a proverb-like text supported by a prose comment; not only are such texts with comments prominent in *Ecclesiasticus* and *Ecclesiastes*, but the form persists to the time of the *Epistle of St. James*. In this form of text and comment the Sermon on the Mount presents seven divisions, elaborating the foundation ideas of the new and heavenly wisdom. The shock of the opening text makes us feel how by the doctrine of Jesus the centre of gravity of human life and character is wholly shifted. It is to the 'poor in spirit' that the exaltation of the new kingdom comes; and this phrase of the text gathers fulness with its sevenfold expansion — the mourners are blessed, and not the gay; the meek, and not the mighty; those who hunger after a righteousness they have not attained, and not the satisfied Pharisee; the merciful, and not the oppressor; the pure and not the worldly; the peacemaker, and not the conqueror; the persecutor is beneath his victim. Again, in contrast with the received ideal of a personal righteousness that would outshine that of others, the second and third maxims, with their images of the salt and the lamp, put forward an exaltation that is exalted only so long as it exerts its purifying and illuminating force upon others. The central article of the discourse brings out that the gospel is no relaxation of the law, but its intensification; the exposi-

Introduction

tion of this thought is the paradox that the new righteousness must exceed the righteousness of Scribes and Pharisees, and its final word is perfection. The fifth article prescribes the heavenward reference of our worship, in contradistinction to the righteousness that would be seen of men; the sixth calls for a heavenward trend of our desires in contradistinction to laying up treasure upon earth. It is in strict accordance with Wisdom literature that the final section should be a series of miscellaneous precepts; and the discourse finds a closing note in the impressive image of the builders on the sand and on the rock.

In the philosophic arrangement of St. Matthew's Gospel the connected teaching of Jesus has been first exhibited, and its consequences remain to be regularly traced. The new doctrine has been, as it were, flung into the still waters of Jewish society; subsequent portions of the narrative watch the widening circles of effect. Or there is a better image to be found in the book itself. John the Baptist, in one of the sayings recorded by Matthew, describes his successor as having a fan in his hand, with which he will throughly purge his floor, gathering the wheat into his garner, and burning the chaff. This image of winnowing the wheat from the chaff seems to underlie the whole story of the developing kingdom of heaven, as St. Matthew tells it: from the first moment there appears an ever-widening rift between those who accept and those who oppose.

In the fifth section of Matthew's narrative, which gives

Introduction

the First Impressions of the teaching of Jesus, the two elements of the coming conflict are seen side by side. There is the Gathering of Disciples: not only are personal calls recorded, but at this point the very Scribes themselves show a disposition to press into the kingdom. There are also Hints of Antagonism, and at this time they are no more than hints: silent doubts as to the claim to forgive sins, respectful questionings as to unpatriotic companying with publicans, or immoral companying with sinners, as to feasting while others fast. The section has an appropriate climax in an incident which leads the multitude to cry out in wonder, and the Pharisees to mutter the thought which hereafter is to be their great blasphemy.

But from this point the winnowing power of Christ's ministry, and the divergent effects of its contact with human society, have so increased that the successive sections of St. Matthew's narrative similarly diverge, and alternately treat of the disciples, with their deepening hold of the kingdom, and the outside world, with its intensifying opposition. The fifth section draws into one view the Organisation of Apostles to spread the news of the kingdom, and similarly unifies the instructions given them into a single Sevenfold Commission. From the Apostles the narrative turns, in the sixth section, to the world, and brings out the Growing Isolation of Jesus in his Ministry: he gradually draws apart from the imperfect ministry of his forerunner; from the Pharisaic doctrine of the Sabbath,

Introduction

the great outward mark of the Hebrew nation; other opposition of the Pharisees is pronounced a blasphemy against the Spirit of Holiness; from the wisdom and might of the great cities he turns to the simplicity of babes, to those who labour and are heavy laden; a final touch is found in the separation of Jesus from his very mother and brethren. With the seventh section we have returned to the band of disciples: here is brought out the distinction between the Public Parable, the dark saying addressed with its own winnowing power to the multitude, and the Private Interpretation, which with unwearied patience gives the full light to those who are thus being initiated into the 'mystery' of the kingdom of heaven. The eighth section resumes the external ministry: here are related the Greater Miracles — the wide-reaching effects of such incidents as the feeding of multitudes with a few loaves and fishes; here equally appears the Growing Antagonism, by which Christ's own country casts him off, and Jerusalem sends a deputation to watch him, while Jesus himself staggers the faith of those closest to him by cutting down at one stroke the whole Tradition of the Elders, which had cast a veil of ceremonial frivolities over the face of the Mosaic law. Section nine, commencing with the confession of Peter, records the Full Recognition by the Disciples of the Kingdom; but the strange doctrine of the sufferings of the Messiah, which is thereupon revealed to them, raises in their minds perplexing questions of the Kingdom, and

Introduction

its spirit is more and more fully unfolded. This brings us to the tenth section, the Entry into Jerusalem, and the Final Breach with the Ruling Classes; it closes with the sevenfold denunciation of the Scribes and Pharisees, and the weeping over the doomed city. The public ministry of Jesus has now closed: the eleventh section contains the Discourse to the Disciples which is the Revelation of the End; and the final division of the narrative records the Passion of Jesus and his Resurrection.

Literary criticism shows at its worst when it seeks to make preferences; and it would be wanting in reverence to the sacred character of the gospels to exalt one above the other. Each has its proper function, and makes appeal to a different class of readers. But it may be said that the *Gospel of St. Matthew* has a special interest for modern thought, and the rational spirit of enquiry which seeks a connected view of even the most sacred incidents; here we have a mind, cast in the mould of Hebrew philosophy, exhibiting its philosophic grasp of an historic world-movement of which the outer form is Hebrew. The historic books of the Old Testament, however much they may leave to critical enquiry for adjustment and reconstruction, make a noble literary whole. They are the story of a theocracy in conflict with the secular: a national sense of divine kingship is gradually dissipated by assimilation to the visible government of surrounding peoples. Thus the Old Testament history is history of

Introduction

failure: the secular government culminates in national exile, and the restored Jewish church becomes spiritual at the price of increased exclusiveness. A truer conclusion to the history of the Old Testament is found in the gospel of St. Matthew: here a kingdom of God that is essentially spiritual is seen developing in conflict with secular powers, which crush out of it all that is not spiritual, eternal, universal. There can be no fitter close for this narrative of St. Matthew than his brief picture of the risen Lord, on the mountain of ascension, giving to the band of disciples the command to make disciples of all the nations, animated by a presence that will be in their midst even to the end of the world.

II

To the *Gospel of St. Mark*, considered as a literary work, little is needed in the way of introduction. It is sufficiently obvious that this gospel is addressed, not to Hebrews, but to Gentiles; and several times parentheses — in modern phrase, footnotes — give explanations of details which by Hebrew readers would be taken for granted. In this, more than in the other narratives, we find general pictures of the ministry of Jesus. Especially prominent is the constant crowding of the multitudes roused by the works of wonder, which drive Jesus into desert places to seek privacy, while, if he enters a house, the whole city is gathered at the door. St. Mark deals much less fully

Introduction

than the other evangelists with the actual teaching of the Master: the very 'Sermon on the Mount' is wanting. On the other hand, he preserves with more minuteness the outward circumstances amid which the teaching is delivered. All three gospels bring out the exceeding difficulty with which the disciples receive the revelation of the sufferings of the Messiah: it is Mark who tells us how on the very mountain of the transfiguration the disciples 'wist not what to answer' and 'became sore afraid'; how again, 'they understood not the saying, and were afraid to ask him'; how, in the going up to Jerusalem, 'Jesus was going before them, and they were amazed, and they that followed were afraid.' St. Matthew makes a single incident of the barren fig tree: St. Mark relates separately the mystic words addressed to the tree, and how, on the following morning, the marvel of the tree's withering drew another lesson from the Master. St. Matthew, with his tendency to classification, includes with the other tempting questions the scribe's enquiry as to the great commandment of the law: St. Mark has preserved the separateness of this from the rest, and how the scribe did homage to the grandeur of the reply, and Jesus recognised the different spirit of this questioner. The external details introduced by this evangelist often serve as links binding incidents together: Matthew relates Christ's saying about his mother and brethren immediately after the blasphemy of the Pharisees, but it is Mark who opens this latter

Introduction

incident with the description of the crowd around the house where Jesus met the Pharisees, which was keeping his brethren outside. Accordingly, every reader catches in *St. Mark* a graphic fulness of detail suggesting that ultimately, if not immediately, this narrative has come from an eye-witness. It is here we read of the healing of a deaf man: how —

> he took him aside from the multitude privately, and put his fingers into his ears, and he spat, and touched his tongue; and looking up to heaven, he sighed, and saith unto him, *Ephphatha*, that is, Be opened.

The healing of Bartimæus, again, is full of graphic detail:

> And many rebuked him, that he should hold his peace: but he cried out the more a great deal, Thou son of David, have mercy on me. And Jesus stood still, and said, Call ye him. And they call the blind man, saying unto him, Be of good cheer: rise, he calleth thee. And he, casting away his garment, sprang up, and came to Jesus.

And the narrative of Mark alone preserves one detail of the arrest — the young man, roused from sleep, with a linen cloth cast hastily on his body, hanging curiously about the procession, until at the first touch of an officer he leaves his garment and flees away naked: a detail of no relevance to the sacred character of the events, but giving a wonderful touch of vivid weirdness to the picture of that moment of panic. The main characteristic of St. Mark

→❸ **Introduction**

then is incidental narration. And this affects the literary form of this gospel. We have here, not the grouping of circumstances by classes or stages, but a sequence of independent narratives: I have not attempted in this case to arrange in organic chapters, but have allowed the whole to stand as a series of separate incidents. *The Gospel of St. Mark* is not to be described as history, but as memoirs.

III

'An Epistle to Hebrews' is a fair rendering of the traditional title, which, though it can have no authority as part of the original document, yet is borne out by the substance of the epistle to which it is prefixed. The epistle is undoubtedly addressed to a particular church, which is specifically described as having once made a worthy confession under stress of persecution, and latterly in danger of relapsing to lower planes of spiritual life. But the address is made to the members of this church in their capacity as Hebrews, and a line of thought is followed which would appeal to the Hebrew mind wherever it was found. The work is thus in the fullest sense an 'Epistle General': a manifesto called forth perhaps by particular circumstances, but exhibiting a general view of Christian truth as regarded from one of its many sides.

Here, as always, full sympathy with a literary work involves clear grasp of its exact form. We are separated

Introduction

from the Epistle to Hebrews, not only by differences of thought, but also by differences in habit and plan of thinking. One of these differences it is easy to formulate. In the introduction to another volume* of this series I have spoken of the peculiar position of the digression in ancient literary style. With us a digression is regarded as an exceptional thing, almost a confession of weakness. With certain writers of antiquity the digression is plainly an end in itself, a distinct element in an artistic scheme of exposition. *The Wisdom of Solomon* — echoes of which are found in *Hebrews* — exhibits a chain of digressions regularly worked out and articulated into a main argument, the digressions sometimes containing the writer's most prominent thoughts. It is the same in a less degree with the work here under consideration. The epistle towards its close speaks of itself as a 'word of exhortation': and there is running through it a strain of exhortation which must be regarded as the main thought. But with this are associated closely reasoned arguments, of the nature of digressions, by which particular points in the exhortation are supported; in this digressive form are elaborated some of the most important among the leading ideas of the epistle, and in actual bulk the digressions make the larger half of the whole work. They are thus not so much digressions as tributary streams of thought; and the exhortation, as it

* *Ecclesiastes* and *Wisdom of Solomon*, page xxiv.

resumes, gathers into the main stream of thought the successive contributions with which its volume is enriched.

The epistle opens with a majestic sentence, in which it is said how the scattered revelations of the prophets have grown into a full revelation through a Son, who after his finished work of purification is exalted to the right hand of God. But before this sentence has reached the word of exhortation up to which it is leading a digression occurs. We are accustomed to think of the Law as given through Moses: the age of this epistle had expanded certain hints of the Old Testament into a complete doctrine of the mediation of angels as associated with the mediation of Moses. Accordingly the mention in the opening sentence of the word 'angels' drives the writer to his first line of tributary argument; by elaborate quotations from Scripture is shown the superiority of the Son to the angels, who are but servants working for the heirs of salvation. Resuming, the main thought exhorts to a greater diligence worthy of the greater salvation, a salvation by one to whom all things are subjected. Another digression anticipates the objection that all things are not yet seen in subjection to Jesus; on the contrary, he has been made 'a little lower than the angels,' but only in order that by suffering he may become a faithful High Priest to mediate between God and a sinful people. In this paragraph of digression has appeared the chief thought in this first of the main divisions of the epistle — the High Priesthood of Jesus.

Introduction

The exhortation, as it resumes, gathers in this thought of the High Priesthood of Jesus; comparing his faithfulness with the faithfulness of God's servant Moses, the writer quotes the psalmist's appeal against the hardening of heart which kept some of Moses's followers from entering into God's rest. This leads to a digression, in which it is argued that the 'rest' which the psalmist has in mind can be neither the rest after the work of creation, nor yet the rest of the promised land: there must remain a sabbath rest for the people of God. The exhortation can then continue: let us hold fast our confession, confiding in our High Priest. This gives opportunity for the advance of thought which makes the second division of the epistle: not only is Jesus High Priest, but his is a priesthood more exalted than that of the Levitical law — he is a High Priest after the order of Melchizedek. The thought thus opened is supported by a series of digressive arguments. First, there is a digression in the full sense of the term: an appeal to the Hebrews addressed in the epistle to rouse themselves from apathy, and press on towards fulness of spiritual growth. Then three lines of analogy are elaborated, bringing out the superior priesthood of the Christ. Melchizedek abides a priest for ever: in contrast with a Levitical order of mortal priests, which indeed, in Abraham, did homage to Melchizedek. Again, Jesus is minister of the true tabernacle, not its shadow: the very ritual of the old dispensation proclaimed that the way to the holiest was not yet manifested, whereas Christ, through the more perfect tabernacle 'not made with hands' passed once for all into the holy place, and made eternal redemption. Yet again, the covenant of Moses needed a victim whose blood was its dedicatory sign: his better sacrifice of himself, and his blood of cleansing, has made Jesus the mediator of a better covenant.

We pass into the third division of the epistle, which gathers up the thoughts of the High Priesthood of Jesus and the way thus opened into the holy place, and makes appeal to hold fast hope and confession, with even more firmness as the end approaches; since it is 'by his faith that the righteous shall live.' This quotation from Habakkuk gives opportunity for the famous digression, in which 'faith' is described as giving substance to future hopes and daring to put the unseen to the test. It displays the long succession of the fathers, who had witness borne to their faith, yet received not the promise, waiting for us before they could be made perfect. When from the digression we return to the appeal, this glorious array of witnesses is made additional incentive to high effort in the race set before us, to an endurance of what is but the pain of chastening. So is reached the peroration: not to the material terrors of Moses's mount have they come, but to the spiritual glories of Mount Zion and the Mediator of the New Covenant. A fourth section of general exhortations brings the epistle to a close.

Introduction ❦

Such is the regular scheme of thought in the Epistle to Hebrews: a strain of exhortation resting upon tributary lines of argument which interrupt it only to enrich. The treatment of this and the other epistles in the present edition will be one which I have already applied in earlier volumes to Wisdom literature: I offer little in the way of notes, but endeavour to bring out the connection of thought through a whole work by a syllabus, constructed on the principle that a paragraph of the syllabus stands for a paragraph of the text. In the present case the two lines of thought that are interwoven throughout the whole movement of the epistle will be found separated to the eye in the syllabus.

IV

The Epistle of St. James, it is manifest to every reader, stands apart from all the other epistles of the New Testament. It contains nothing of an epistle except the superscription; for the rest, both matter and form assimilate its contents to the scriptural philosophy which is called Wisdom literature. In place of the connected thread of argument making the unity of a Pauline epistle we have in this work independent sections: these are found to be in form maxims and essays of the type of *Ecclesiasticus*. Of this last work St. James is clearly a deep student. *The Wisdom of Jesus the son of Sirach* in the Old Testament Apocrypha has its counterpart in *The Wisdom of St.*

Introduction

James in the New Testament. It is true that two out of the twelve portions into which this epistle may be divided are cast in the more direct form of appeal which makes them discourses; but the work in this respect is not going beyond the range of gnomic literature as seen in *The Wisdom of Solomon*. The matter of this book represents the old conception of Wisdom leavened with the new spirit of Christianity. It is significant that the universal formula of Old Testament wisdom, 'My Son,' is here replaced by the 'My brethren' that still greets us from Christian pulpits. St. James's topics are just what the combination of the Old and the New would suggest. He expounds the paradox of the Joy of Temptation, of the brother of low degree glorying in his high estate and the rich in that he is made low; he speaks of the Prayer for Wisdom, Respect of Persons, Faith and Works, the Responsibility of Speech, the Earthly Wisdom and the Wisdom from Above, the Blessed Work of Converting. If 'the law' is all in all to the son of Sirach, St. James stands no less for the supremacy of the Christian 'law of liberty.' Perhaps the profoundest reflection in all Wisdom literature is the essay in which St. James is enquiring into the Sources of the Evil and the Good in us: of the Evil, in the chain of degeneration through the three links lust, sin, death; of the good, in the inborn word developed by patient listening and acting until it can look into the perfect mirror of the law of liberty. And in considering this essay as a literary

Introduction

work, it becomes not less interesting when we recollect that it has inspired the allegory of Sin and Death, which makes one of the strongest threads running through the *Paradise Lost* of Milton.

V

There remain in the contents of this miscellaneous volume three more works: the Epistles of St. Peter and St. Jude. These belong to the type already mentioned — the Epistle General. In two out of the three the superscription makes them universal; in the other case St. Peter addresses the Elect of a Dispersion so wide as to be practically universal. The contents of the three have the character that belongs to the General Epistle: they are manifestos of the whole Christian faith, modified in its presentation by the special circumstances which call them forth. In all three these surrounding circumstances are the same: a near sense of the end of all things, and the intrusion of false prophets who are corrupting the church from purity of doctrine and of living.

The matter of the three epistles I endeavour to bring out in the form of a syllabus such as I have already described. One remark may be added here. No one can read *St. Peter* and *St. Jude* without feeling that a stream of fervid eloquence runs through each. Yet in their English dress the eloquence of these writings suffers interrup-

Introduction

tion through the way in which successive sentences are dovetailed together with a roughness that often seems awkwardness. Partly no doubt this arises from real divergence in habits of thought between our times and the times of the epistles. But in part I believe the apparent obscurity of these works may be credited to received theories of translation, according to which every Greek particle must have a representation in the wording of the English sentence. In concatenation of sentences the Greek and English languages are strongly contrasted: Greek prose packs its sentences into close connection by the positive bonds of particles; the English, more than most languages, leans to asyndeton. It is too often assumed that Greek in this respect has a logical superiority, which the English translator seeks as far as may be to imitate. But this may reasonably be doubted. In art it is recognised that to suggest is often more potent than to define; and the genius of the English language, that allows sentences to suggest their mutual relations without the interference of a visible symbol of connection, may be more true to the subtleties of thought than the Greek habit of indicating connection by words, which soon become more defined than the relations for which they have to stand. We may yet hope to see translation that would leave such writings as *St. Peter* and *St. Jude* to exert the full power of their eloquence, uninterrupted by repeated strains of what is to us unnatural sentence connection.

Introduction ⁂

⁂

The text is that of the Revised Version, the marginal alternatives being often adopted. For the use of it I express my obligation to the University Presses of Oxford and Cambridge. A Reference Table at the end connects the numbering of this volume with the chapters and verses of the Bible.

THE GOOD TIDINGS
(GOSPEL)

OR

THE ACTS AND SAYINGS OF JESUS

ACCORDING TO

ST. MATTHEW

St. Matthew

I
THE BIRTH OF JESUS

II
JOHN THE BAPTIST AND THE APPEARANCE OF JESUS IN PUBLIC

III
OPENING OF THE MINISTRY OF JESUS AND THE SEVENFOLD DISCOURSE

IV
FIRST IMPRESSIONS: GATHERING OF DISCIPLES AND HINTS OF ANTAGONISM

V
ORGANISATION OF APOSTLES AND THE SEVENFOLD COMMISSION

VI
GROWING ISOLATION OF JESUS AND HIS MINISTRY

St. Matthew

VII
THE PUBLIC PARABLE AND THE PRIVATE INTERPRETATION

VIII
THE GREATER MIRACLES AND THE GROWING ANTAGONISM

IX
FULLER RECOGNITION BY THE DISCIPLES OF THE KINGDOM AND QUESTIONS ARISING THEREUPON

X
THE ENTRY INTO JERUSALEM AND FINAL BREACH WITH THE RULING CLASSES

XI
DISCOURSE TO THE DISCIPLES: THE SEVENFOLD REVELATION OF THE END

XII
THE PASSION AND RESURRECTION OF JESUS

The Genealogy of Jesus Christ
the Son of David
the Son of Abraham

Genealogy → **The Gospel**

Abraham begat Isaac
  and Isaac begat Jacob
    and Jacob begat Judah and his brethren
      and Judah begat Perez and Zerah of Tamar
        and Perez begat Hezron
          and Hezron begat Ram
            and Ram begat Amminadab
              and Amminadab begat Nahshon
                and Nahshon begat Salmon
                  and Salmon begat Boaz of Rahab
                    and Boaz begat Obed of Ruth
                      and Obed begat Jesse
                        and Jesse begat David the King.

And David begat Solomon of her that had been the wife of Uriah
  and Solomon begat Rehoboam
    and Rehoboam begat Abijah
      and Abijah begat Asa
        and Asa begat Jehoshaphat
          and Jehoshaphat begat Joram
            and Joram begat Uzziah
              and Uzziah begat Jotham
                and Jotham begat Ahaz
                  and Ahaz begat Hezekiah
                    and Hezekiah begat Manasseh
                      and Manasseh begat Amon
                        and Amon begat Josiah
                          and Josiah begat Jechoniah and his brethren at the time of the carrying away to Babylon.

St. Matthew   Genealogy

And after the carrying away to Babylon Jechoniah begat Shealtiel
  and Shealtiel begat Zerubbabel
    and Zerubbabel begat Abiud
      and Abiud begat Eliakim
        and Eliakim begat Azor
          and Azor begat Sadoc
            and Sadoc begat Achim
              and Achim begat Eliud
                and Eliud begat Eleazar
                  and Eleazar begat Matthan
                    and Matthan begat Jacob
                      and Jacob begat Joseph
                        the husband of Mary
                          of whom was born Jesus who is
                          called the Christ.

So all the generations from Abraham unto David are fourteen generations

    and from David unto the carrying away to Babylon fourteen generations

        and from the carrying away to Babylon unto the Christ fourteen generations.

I

THE BIRTH OF JESUS

Now the birth of Jesus Christ was on this wise: When his mother Mary had been betrothed to Joseph, before they came together she was found with child of the Holy Ghost. And Joseph her husband, being a righteous man, and not willing to make her a public example, was minded to put her away privily. But when he thought on these things, behold, an angel of the Lord appeared unto him in a dream, saying, Joseph, thou son of David, fear not to take unto thee Mary thy wife: for that which is conceived in her is of the Holy Ghost. And she shall bring forth a son; and thou shalt call his name

Birth of Jesus

JESUS

for it is he that shall 'save' his people from their sins. Now all this is come to pass, that it might be fulfilled which was spoken by the Lord through the prophet, saying: *Behold, the virgin shall be with child, and shall bring forth a son, and they shall call his name 'Immanuel';*

I   The Gospel

which is, being interpreted, 'God with us.' And Joseph arose from his sleep, and did as the angel of the Lord commanded him, and took unto him his wife; and knew her not till she had brought forth a son: and he called his name

JESUS.

Now when Jesus was born in Bethlehem of Judæa in the days of Herod the king, behold, Wise men from the east **Visit of the Magi—Flight into Egypt** came to Jerusalem, saying, Where is he that is born King of the Jews? for we saw his star in the east, and are come to worship him. And when Herod the king heard it, he was troubled, and all Jerusalem with him. And gathering together all the chief priests and scribes of the people, he inquired of them where the Christ should be born. And they said unto him, In Bethlehem of Judæa: for thus it is written by the prophet: *And thou Bethlehem, land of Judah, art in no wise least among the princes of Judah: for out of thee shall come forth a governor, which shall be shepherd of my people Israel.* Then Herod privily called the Wise men, and learned of them carefully what time the star appeared. And he sent them to Bethlehem, and said, Go and search out carefully concerning the young child; and when ye have found him, bring me word, that I also may come and worship him. And they, having heard the king, went their way; and lo, the star, which they saw in the east, went before them, till it came and stood over where the young child was. And when they saw the star, they rejoiced with exceeding great joy. And they came into the house and saw the young child with Mary his mother; and they fell down and worshipped him; and opening their treasures they offered unto him gifts, gold and frankincense and myrrh. And being warned of God in a dream that they should not return to Herod, they departed into their own country another way.

Now when they were departed, behold, an angel of the Lord appeareth to Joseph in a dream, saying, Arise and take the young child and his mother, and flee into Egypt, and be thou there until I tell thee: for Herod will seek the young child to destroy him. And he arose and took the young child and his mother by night, and departed into Egypt; and was there until the death of Herod: that it might be fulfilled which was spoken by the Lord through the prophet, saying, *Out of Egypt did I call my son.* Then Herod, when he saw that he was mocked of the Wise men, was exceeding wroth, and sent forth, and slew all the male children that were in Bethlehem, and in all the borders thereof, from two years old and under, according to the time which he had carefully learned of the Wise men. Then was fulfilled that which was spoken by Jeremiah the prophet, saying: *A voice was heard in Ramah, weeping and great mourning, Rachel weeping for her children; and she would not be comforted, because they are not.*

But when Herod was dead, behold, an angel of the Lord appeareth in a dream to Joseph in Egypt, saying, Arise and take the young child and his mother, and go into the land of Israel: for they are dead that sought the young child's life. And he arose and took the young child and his mother, and came into the land of Israel. But when he heard that Archelaus was reigning over Judæa in the room of his father Herod, he was afraid to go thither; and being warned of God in a dream, he withdrew into the parts of Galilee, and came and dwelt in a city called Nazareth: that it might be fulfilled which was spoken by the prophets, that he should be called a Nazarene.

II

JOHN THE BAPTIST AND THE APPEARANCE OF JESUS IN PUBLIC

And in those days cometh John the Baptist, preaching in the wilderness of Judæa, saying, Repent ye; for the kingdom of heaven is at hand. For this is he that was spoken of by Isaiah the prophet, saying: *The voice of one crying in the wilderness, Make ye ready the way of the Lord, make his paths straight.* Now John himself had his raiment of camel's hair, and a leathern girdle about his loins; and his food was locusts and wild honey. Then went out unto him Jerusalem, and all Judæa, and all the region round about Jordan; and they were baptized of him in the river Jordan, confessing their sins. But when he saw many of the Pharisees and Sadducees coming to his baptism, he said unto them, Ye offspring of vipers, who warned you to flee from the wrath to come? Bring forth therefore fruit worthy of repentance: and think not to say within yourselves, We have Abraham to our father: for I say unto you, that God

<small>John the Baptist</small>

is able of these stones to raise up children unto Abraham. And even now is the axe laid unto the root of the trees: every tree therefore that bringeth not forth good fruit is hewn down, and cast into the fire. I indeed baptize you with water unto repentance: but he that cometh after me is mightier than I, whose shoes I am not worthy to bear: he shall baptize you with the Holy Ghost and with fire: whose fan is in his hand, and he will throughly cleanse his threshing-floor; and he will gather his wheat into the garner, but the chaff he will burn up with unquenchable fire.

Then cometh Jesus from Galilee to the Jordan unto John, to be baptized of him. But John would have hindered him, saying, I have need to be baptized of thee, and comest thou to me? But Jesus answering said unto him, Suffer me now: for thus it becometh us to fulfil all righteousness. Then he suffereth him. And Jesus, when he was baptized, went up straightway from the water: and lo, the heavens were opened unto him, and he saw the Spirit of God descending as a dove, and coming upon him; and lo, a voice out of the heavens, saying, This is my beloved Son, in whom I am well pleased.

The Baptism of Jesus

Then was Jesus led up of the Spirit into the wilderness to be tempted of the devil. And when he had fasted forty days and forty nights, he afterward hungered. And the tempter came and said unto him, If thou art the Son of

St. Matthew II

God, command that these stones become bread. But he answered and said, It is written, *Man shall not live by bread alone, but by every word that proceedeth out of the mouth of God.* Then the devil taketh him into the holy city; and he set him on the pinnacle of the temple, and saith unto him, If thou art the Son of God, cast thyself down: for it is written,

The Temptation in the Wilderness

> *He shall give his angels charge concerning thee:*
> *And on their hands they shall bear thee up,*
> *Lest haply thou dash thy foot against a stone.*

Jesus said unto him, Again it is written, *Thou shalt not tempt the Lord thy God.* Again, the devil taketh him unto an exceeding high mountain, and sheweth him all the kingdoms of the world, and the glory of them; and he said unto him, All these things will I give thee, if thou wilt fall down and worship me. Then saith Jesus unto him, Get thee hence, Satan: for it is written, *Thou shalt worship the Lord thy God, and him only shalt thou serve.* Then the devil leaveth him; and behold, angels came and ministered unto him.

Now when he heard that John was delivered up, he withdrew into Galilee; and leaving Nazareth, he came and dwelt in Capernaum, which is by the sea, in the borders of Zebulun and Naphtali: that it might be fulfilled which was spoken by Isaiah the prophet, saying:

The land of Zebulun and the land of Naphtali,
Toward the sea, beyond Jordan, Galilee of the Gentiles,
The people which sat in darkness
Saw a great light,
And to them which sat in the region and shadow of death,
To them did light spring up.

III

OPENING OF THE MINISTRY OF JESUS AND THE SEVENFOLD DISCOURSE

From that time began Jesus to preach, and to say, Repent ye; for the kingdom of heaven is at hand.

And walking by the sea of Galilee, he saw two brethren, Simon who is called Peter, and Andrew his brother, casting a net into the sea; for they were fishers. And he saith unto them, Come ye after me, and I will make you fishers of men. And they straightway left the nets, and followed him. And going on from thence he saw other two brethren, James the son of Zebedee, and John his brother, in the boat with Zebedee their father, mending their nets; and he called them. And they straightway left the boat and their father, and followed him.

And Jesus went about in all Galilee, teaching in their synagogues, and preaching the gospel of the kingdom, and healing all manner of disease and all manner of sickness among the people. And the report of him went forth into all Syria: and they brought unto him all that were sick, holden with divers diseases and torments, possessed with devils, and epileptic, and palsied; and he healed them. And there followed him great multitudes from Galilee and Decapolis and Jerusalem and Judæa and from beyond Jordan.

And seeing the multitudes, he went up into the mountain: and when he had sat down, his disciples came unto him: and he opened his mouth and taught them, saying:

i

Blessed are the poor in spirit:
For theirs is the kingdom of heaven.

Blessed are they that mourn: for they shall be comforted. Blessed are the meek: for they shall inherit the earth. Blessed are they that hunger and thirst after righteousness: for they shall be filled. Blessed are the merciful: for they shall obtain mercy. Blessed are the pure in heart: for they shall see God. Blessed are the peacemakers: for they shall be called sons of God. Blessed are they that have been persecuted for righteousness' sake: for theirs is the kingdom of heaven. Blessed are ye when men shall reproach you, and persecute you, and say all manner of evil against you falsely, for my sake. Rejoice, and be exceeding glad: for great is your reward in heaven: for so persecuted they the prophets which were before you.

ii

Ye are the salt of the earth.

But if the salt have lost its savour, wherewith shall it be salted? it is thenceforth good for nothing, but to be cast out and trodden under foot of men.

iii

Ye are the light of the world.

A city set on a hill cannot be hid. Neither do men light a lamp, and put it under the bushel, but on the stand; and it shineth unto all that are in the house. Even so let your light shine before men, that they may see your good works, and glorify your Father which is in heaven.

iv

Think not that I came to destroy the law or the prophets: I came not to destroy, but to fulfil.

For verily I say unto you, Till heaven and earth pass away, one jot or one tittle shall in no wise pass away from the law, till all things be accomplished. Whosoever therefore shall break one of these least commandments, and shall teach men so, shall be called least in the kingdom of heaven: but whosoever shall do and teach them, he shall be called great in the kingdom of heaven.

For I say unto you, that except your righteousness shall exceed the righteousness of the scribes and Pharisees, ye shall in no wise enter into the kingdom of heaven. Ye have heard that it was said to them of old time, Thou shalt not kill; and whosoever shall kill shall be in danger of the judgement: but I say unto you, that every one who is angry with his brother shall be in danger of the judgement; and whosoever shall say to his brother, Raca, shall be in danger of the council; and whosoever shall say, Thou fool, shall be in danger of the hell of fire. If therefore thou art offering thy gift at the altar, and there rememberest that thy brother hath aught against thee, leave there thy gift before the altar, and go thy way, first be reconciled to thy brother, and then come and offer thy gift. Agree with thine adversary quickly, whiles thou art with him in the way; lest haply the adversary deliver thee to the judge, and the judge deliver thee to the officer, and thou be cast into prison: verily I say unto thee, Thou shalt by no means come out thence, till thou have paid the last farthing. Ye have heard that it was said, Thou shalt not commit adultery: but I say unto you, that every one that looketh on a woman to lust after her hath committed adultery with her already in his heart. And if thy right eye causeth thee to stumble, pluck it out, and cast it from thee: for it is profitable for thee that one of thy members should perish, and not thy whole body be cast into hell. And if thy right hand causeth thee to stumble, cut it off, and cast it from thee: for it is profitable for thee that one of thy members should perish, and not thy whole body go into hell. It was said also, Whosoever shall put away his wife, let him give her a writing of divorcement: but I say unto you, that every one that putteth away his wife, saving for the cause of fornication, maketh her an adulteress: and whosoever shall marry her when she is put away committeth adultery. Again, ye have heard that it was said to them of old time, Thou shalt not forswear thyself, but shalt perform unto the Lord thine oaths: but I say unto you, Swear not at all; neither by the heaven, for it is the throne of God; nor by the earth, for it is the footstool of his feet; nor by Jerusalem, for it is the city of the great King; neither shalt thou swear by thy head, for thou canst not make one hair white or black. But let your speech be, Yea, yea; Nay, nay: and whatsoever is more than these is of the evil one. Ye have heard that it was said, An eye for an eye, and a tooth for a tooth: but I say unto you, Resist not him that is evil: but whosoever smiteth thee on thy right cheek, turn to him the other also. And if any man would go to law with thee, and take away thy coat, let him have thy cloke also. And whosoever shall compel thee to go one mile, go with him twain. Give to him that asketh thee, and from him that would borrow of thee turn not thou away. Ye have heard that it was said,

Thou shalt love thy neighbour, and hate thine enemy: but I say unto you, Love your enemies, and pray for them that persecute you; that ye may be sons of your Father which is in heaven: for he maketh his sun to rise on the evil and the good, and sendeth rain on the just and the unjust. For if ye love them that love you, what reward have ye? do not even the publicans the same? And if ye salute your brethren only, what do ye more than others? do not even the Gentiles the same? Ye therefore shall be perfect, as your heavenly Father is perfect.

V

Take heed that ye do not your righteousness before men,
    to be seen of them:
Else ye have no reward with your Father which is in
    heaven.

When therefore thou doest alms, sound not a trumpet before thee, as the hypocrites do in the synagogues and in the streets, that they may have glory of men. Verily I say unto you, They have received their reward. But when thou doest alms, let not thy left hand know what thy right hand doeth: that thine alms may be in secret: and thy Father which seeth in secret shall recompense thee. And when ye pray, ye shall not be as the hypocrites: for they love to stand and pray in the synagogues

St. Matthew

and in the corners of the streets, that they may be seen of men. Verily I say unto you, They have received their reward. But thou, when thou prayest, enter into thine inner chamber, and having shut thy door, pray to thy Father which is in secret, and thy Father which seeth in secret shall recompense thee. And in praying use not vain repetitions, as the Gentiles do: for they think that they shall be heard for their much speaking. Be not therefore like unto them: for your Father knoweth what things ye have need of, before ye ask him. After this manner therefore pray ye:

> Our Father which art in heaven:
>   Hallowed be thy name,
>   Thy kingdom come,
>   Thy will be done,
> As in heaven, so on earth.
>
> Give us this day
> Our daily bread.
>
> And forgive us our debts,
> As we also have forgiven our debtors.
>
> And bring us not into temptation,
> But deliver us from the evil one.

For if ye forgive men their trespasses, your heavenly Father will also forgive you. But if ye forgive not men their trespasses, neither will your Father forgive your trespasses. Moreover when ye fast, be not, as the hypocrites, of a sad countenance: for they disfigure their faces, that they may be seen of men to fast. Verily I say unto you, They have received their reward. But thou, when thou fastest, anoint thy head, and wash thy face; that thou be not seen of men to fast, but of thy Father which is in secret: and thy Father, which seeth in secret, shall recompense thee.

vi

Lay not up for yourselves treasures upon the earth,
   Where moth and rust doth consume,
   And where thieves break through and steal:
But lay up for yourselves treasures in heaven,
   Where neither moth nor rust doth consume,
   And where thieves do not break through nor steal.

For where thy treasure is, there will thy heart be also. The lamp of the body is the eye: if therefore thine eye be single, thy whole body shall be full of light; but if thine eye be evil, thy whole body shall be full of darkness; if therefore the light that is in thee be darkness, how great is the darkness! No man can serve two masters: for either he will hate the one, and love the other; or else he will hold to one, and despise the other. Ye cannot serve God and mammon. Therefore I say unto you, be not anxious for your life, what ye shall eat, or what ye shall drink; nor yet for your body, what ye shall put on. Is not the life more than the food, and the body than the raiment? Behold the birds of the heaven, that they sow not, neither do they reap, nor gather into barns; and your heavenly Father feedeth them. Are not ye of much more value than they? And which of you by being anxious can add one cubit unto his stature? And why are ye anxious concerning raiment? Consider the lilies of the field, how they grow; they toil not, neither do they spin: yet I say unto you, that even Solomon in all his glory was not arrayed like one of these. But if God doth so clothe the grass of the field, which today is, and tomorrow is cast into the oven, shall he not much more clothe you, O ye of little faith? Be not therefore anxious, saying, What shall we eat? or, What shall we drink? or, Wherewithal shall we be clothed?—for after all these things do the Gentiles seek—for your heavenly Father knoweth that ye have need of all these things. But seek ye first his kingdom, and his righteousness; and all these things shall be added unto you. Be not therefore anxious for the morrow: for the morrow will be anxious for itself. Sufficient unto the day is the evil thereof.

vii

1

Judge not:
That ye be not judged.

For with what judgement ye judge, ye shall be judged: and with what measure ye mete, it shall be measured unto you. And why beholdest thou the mote that is in thy brother's eye, but considerest not the beam that is in thine own eye? Or how wilt thou say to thy brother, Let me cast out the mote out of thine eye; and lo, the beam is in thine own eye? Thou hypocrite, cast out first the beam out of thine own eye; and then shalt thou see clearly to cast out the mote out of thy brother's eye.

2

Give not that which is holy unto the dogs,
   Neither cast your pearls before the swine:
     Lest haply they trample them under their feet,
And turn and rend you.

3

Ask, and it shall be given you;
   Seek, and ye shall find;
     Knock, and it shall be opened unto you:
For every one that asketh receiveth,
   And he that seeketh findeth,
     And to him that knocketh it shall be opened.

Or what man is there of you, who, if his son shall ask him for a loaf, will give him a stone; or if he shall ask for a fish, will give him a serpent? If ye then, being evil, know how to give good gifts unto your children, how much more shall your Father which is in heaven give good things to them that ask him?

4

All things therefore whatsoever ye would that men should do unto you, even so do ye also unto them: for this is the law and the prophets.

5

Enter ye in by the narrow gate.

For wide is the gate, and broad is the way, that leadeth to destruction, and many be they that enter in thereby. For narrow is the gate, and straitened the way, that leadeth unto life, and few be they that find it.

6

Beware of false prophets,
    Which come to you in sheep's clothing,
    But inwardly are ravening wolves.

By their fruits ye shall know them. Do men gather grapes of thorns, or figs of thistles? Even so every good tree bringeth forth good fruit; but the corrupt tree bringeth

III vii → The Gospel

forth evil fruit. A good tree cannot bring forth evil fruit, neither can a corrupt tree bring forth good fruit. Every tree that bringeth not forth good fruit is hewn down, and cast into the fire. Therefore by their fruits ye shall know them.

7

Not every one that saith unto me, Lord, Lord, shall enter into the kingdom of heaven; but he that doeth the will of my Father which is in heaven. Many will say to me in that day, Lord, Lord, did we not prophesy by thy name, and by thy name cast out devils, and by thy name do many mighty works? And then will I profess unto them, I never knew you: depart from me, ye that work iniquity. Every one therefore which heareth these words of mine, and doeth them, shall be likened unto a wise man, which built his house upon the rock: and the rain descended, and the floods came, and the winds blew, and beat upon that house; and it fell not: for it was founded upon the rock. And every one that heareth these words of mine, and doeth them not, shall be likened unto a foolish man, which built his house upon the sand: and the rain descended, and the floods came, and the winds blew, and smote upon that house; and it fell: and great was the fall thereof.

IV

FIRST IMPRESSIONS: GATHERING OF DISCIPLES AND HINTS OF ANTAGONISM

i

And it came to pass, when Jesus ended these words, the multitudes were astonished at his teaching: for he taught them as one having authority, and not as their scribes.

And when he was come down from the mountain, great multitudes followed him. And behold, there came to him a leper and worshipped him, saying, Lord, if thou wilt, thou canst make me clean. And he stretched forth his hand, and touched him, saying, I will; be thou made clean. And straightway his leprosy was cleansed. And Jesus saith unto him, See thou tell no man; but go thy way, shew thyself to the priest, and offer the gift that Moses commanded, for a testimony unto them.

And when he was entered into Capernaum, there came unto him a centurion, beseeching him, and saying, Lord, my servant lieth in the house sick of the palsy, grievously tormented. And he saith unto him, I will come and heal

IV i — The Gospel

him. And the centurion answered and said, Lord, I am not worthy that thou shouldest come under my roof: but only say the word, and my servant shall be healed. For I also am a man under authority, having under myself soldiers: and I say to this one, Go, and he goeth; and to another, Come, and he cometh; and to my servant, Do this, and he doeth it. And when Jesus heard it, he marvelled, and said to them that followed, Verily I say unto you, I have not found so great faith, no, not in Israel. **And I say unto you, that many shall come from the east and the west, and shall sit down with Abraham, and Isaac, and Jacob, in the kingdom of heaven: but the sons of the kingdom shall be cast forth into the outer darkness: there shall be the weeping and gnashing of teeth.** And Jesus said unto the centurion, Go thy way; as thou hast believed, so be it done unto thee. And the servant was healed in that hour.

<small>The Centurion and the Sons of the kingdom</small>

And when Jesus was come into Peter's house, he saw his wife's mother lying sick of a fever. And he touched her hand, and the fever left her; and she arose, and ministered unto him. And when even was come, they brought unto him many possessed with devils: and he cast out the spirits with a word, and healed all that were sick: that it might be fulfilled which was spoken by Isaiah the prophet, saying, *Himself took our infirmities, and bare our diseases.*

Now when Jesus saw great multitudes about him, he

gave commandment to depart unto the other side. And there came a scribe, and said unto him, Master, I will follow thee whithersoever thou goest. And Jesus saith unto him, **The foxes have holes, and the birds of the heaven have nests; but the Son of man hath not where to lay his head.** And another of the disciples said unto him, Lord, suffer me first to go and bury my father. But Jesus saith unto him, **Follow me; and leave the dead to bury their own dead.**

ii

And when he was entered into a boat, his disciples followed him. And behold, there arose a great tempest in the sea, insomuch that the boat was covered with the waves: but he was asleep. And they came to him, and awoke him, saying, Save, Lord; we perish. And he saith unto them, Why are ye fearful, O ye of little faith? Then he arose, and rebuked the winds and the sea; and there was a great calm. And the men marvelled, saying, What manner of man is this, that even the winds and the sea obey him?

And when he was come to the other side into the country of the Gadarenes, there met him two possessed with devils, coming forth out of the tombs, exceeding fierce, so that no man could pass by that way. And behold, they cried out, saying, What have we to do with thee, thou Son of God? art thou come hither to torment us before the time? Now there was afar off from them a herd of many swine feeding. And the devils besought him, saying, If thou cast us out, send us away into the herd of swine. And he said unto them, Go. And they came out, and went into the swine: and behold, the whole herd rushed down the steep into the sea, and perished in the waters.

<small>A whole city offended</small>
And they that fed them fled, and went away into the city, and told everything, and what was befallen to them that were possessed with devils. And behold, all the city came out to meet Jesus: and when they saw him, they besought him that he would depart from their borders.

iii

And he entered into a boat, and crossed over, and came into his own city. And behold, they brought to him a man sick of the palsy, lying on a bed: and Jesus seeing
<small>Questionings as to Forgiveness of Sins</small>
their faith said unto the sick of the palsy, Son, be of good cheer; thy sins are forgiven. And behold, certain of the scribes said within themselves, This man blasphemeth. And Jesus knowing their thoughts said, Wherefore think ye evil in your hearts? For whether is easier, to say, Thy sins are forgiven; or to say, Arise, and walk? But that ye may know that the Son of man hath power on earth to forgive sins (then saith he to the sick of the palsy), Arise,

and take up thy bed, and go unto thy house. And he arose, and departed to his house. But when the multitudes saw it, they were afraid, and glorified God, which had given such power unto men.

And as Jesus passed by from thence, he saw a man, called Matthew, sitting at the place of toll: and he saith unto him, Follow me. And he arose, and followed him. And it came to pass, as he sat at meat in the house, behold, many publicans and sinners came and sat down with Jesus and his disciples. And when the Pharisees saw it, they said unto his disciples, *As to Company with Sinners* Why eateth your Master with the publicans and sinners? But when he heard it, he said, They that are whole have no need of a physician, but they that are sick. But go ye and learn what this meaneth, I desire mercy, and not sacrifice: for I came not to call the righteous, but sinners.

Then come to him the disciples of John, saying, Why do we and the Pharisees fast oft, but thy disciples fast not? And Jesus said unto them: Can the sons of the bridechamber mourn, as long as *As to Fasting* the bridegroom is with them? but the days will come, when the bridegroom shall be taken away from them, and then will they fast. And no man putteth a piece of undressed cloth upon an old garment; for that which should fill it up taketh from the garment, and a worse rent is made. Neither do men put new wine into old wine-skins:

else the skins burst, and the wine is spilled, and the skins perish: but they put new wine into fresh wine-skins, and both are preserved.

iv

While he spake these things unto them, behold, there came a ruler, and worshipped him, saying, My daughter is even now dead: but come and lay thy hand upon her, and she shall live. And Jesus arose, and followed him, and so did his disciples. And behold, a woman, who had an issue of blood twelve years, came behind him, and touched the border of his garment: for she said within herself, If I do but touch his garment, I shall be made whole. But Jesus turning and seeing her said, Daughter, be of good cheer; thy faith hath made thee whole. And the woman was made whole from that hour. And when Jesus came into the ruler's house, and saw the flute-players, and the crowd making a tumult, he said, Give place: for the damsel is not dead, but sleepeth. And they laughed him to scorn. But when the crowd was put forth, he entered in, and took her by the hand; and the damsel arose. And the fame hereof went forth into all that land.

And as Jesus passed by from thence, two blind men followed him, crying out, and saying, Have mercy on us, thou son of David. And when he was come into the house, the blind men came to him: and Jesus saith unto them, Believe ye that I am able to do this? They say unto him, Yea, Lord. Then touched he their eyes, saying, According to your faith be it done unto you. And their eyes were opened. And Jesus sternly charged them, saying, See that no man know it. But they went forth, and spread abroad his fame in all that land.

And as they went forth, behold, there was brought to him a dumb man possessed with a devil. And when the devil was cast out, the dumb man spake: and the multitudes marvelled, saying, It was never so seen in Israel. But the Pharisees said, By the prince of the devils casteth he out devils.

V

ORGANISATION OF APOSTLES AND THE SEVENFOLD COMMISSION

And Jesus went about all the cities and the villages, teaching in their synagogues, and preaching the gospel of the kingdom, and healing all manner of disease and all manner of sickness. But when he saw the multitudes, he was moved with compassion for them, because they were distressed and scattered, as sheep not having a shepherd. Then saith he unto his disciples, **The harvest truly is plenteous, but the labourers are few. Pray ye therefore the Lord of the harvest, that he send forth labourers into his harvest.**

And he called unto him his twelve disciples, and gave them authority over unclean spirits, to cast them out, and to heal all manner of disease and all manner of sickness. Now the names of the twelve apostles are these: The first, Simon, who is called Peter, and Andrew his brother; James the son of Zebedee, and John his brother; Philip,

St. Matthew V

and Bartholomew; Thomas, and Matthew the publican; 'James the son of Alphæus, and Thaddæus; Simon the Cananæan, and Judas Iscariot, who also betrayed him. These twelve Jesus sent forth, and charged them, saying:

1. Go not into any way of the Gentiles, and enter not into any city of the Samaritans: but go rather to the lost sheep of the house of Israel.

2. And as ye go, preach, saying, The kingdom of heaven is at hand. Heal the sick, raise the dead, cleanse the lepers, cast out devils.

3. Freely ye received, freely give.

4. Get you no gold, nor silver, nor brass in your purses; no wallet for your journey, neither two coats, nor shoes, nor staff: for the labourer is worthy of his food. And into whatsoever city or village ye shall enter, search out who in it is worthy; and there abide till ye go forth. And as ye enter into the house, salute it. And if the house be worthy, let your peace come upon it: but if it be not worthy, let your peace return to you. And whosoever shall not receive you, nor hear your words, as ye go forth out of that house or that city, shake off the dust of your feet. Verily I say unto you, It shall be more tolerable for the land of Sodom and Gomorrah in the day of judgement, than for that city.

5. Behold, I send you forth as sheep in the midst of

wolves: be ye therefore wise as serpents, and harmless as doves. But beware of men: for they will deliver you up to councils, and in their synagogues they will scourge you; yea and before governors and kings shall ye be brought for my sake, for a testimony to them and to the Gentiles. But when they deliver you up, be not anxious how or what ye shall speak: for it shall be given you in that hour what ye shall speak: for it is not ye that speak, but the Spirit of your Father that speaketh in you. And brother shall deliver up brother to death, and the father his child: and children shall rise up against parents, and cause them to be put to death. And ye shall be hated of all men for my name's sake: but he that endureth to the end, the same shall be saved. But when they persecute you in this city, flee into the next: for verily I say unto you, Ye shall not have gone through the cities of Israel, till the Son of man be come. A disciple is not above his master, nor a servant above his lord; it is enough for the disciple that he be as his master, and the servant as his lord: if they have called the master of the house Beelzebub, how much more shall they call them of his household! Fear them not therefore. For there is nothing covered, that shall not be revealed; and hid, that shall not be known: what I tell you in the darkness, speak ye in the light; and what ye hear in the ear, proclaim upon the housetops. And be not afraid of them which kill the body, but are not able to kill the soul: but rather fear him which is able to destroy both soul and body in hell. Are not two sparrows sold for a farthing? and not one of them shall fall on the ground without your Father: but the very hairs of your head are all numbered. Fear not therefore; ye are of more value than many sparrows. Every one therefore who shall confess me before men, him will I also confess before my Father which is in heaven. But whosoever shall deny me before men, him will I also deny before my Father which is in heaven.

6. Think not that I came to send peace on the earth: I came not to send peace, but a sword. For I came to set a man at variance against his father, and the daughter against her mother, and the daughter in law against her mother in law: and a man's foes shall be they of his own household. He that loveth father or mother more than me is not worthy of me; and he that loveth son or daughter more than me is not worthy of me. And he that doth not take his cross and follow after me, is not worthy of me. He that findeth his life shall lose it; and he that loseth his life for my sake shall find it.

7. He that receiveth you receiveth me, and he that receiveth me receiveth him that sent me. He that receiveth a prophet in the name of a prophet shall receive a prophet's reward; and he that receiveth a righteous man in the name of a righteous man shall receive a righteous man's reward. And whosoever shall give to drink unto one of these little ones a cup of cold water only, in the

name of a disciple, verily I say unto you, he shall in no wise lose his reward.

And it came to pass, when Jesus had made an end of commanding his twelve disciples, he departed thence to teach and preach in their cities.

St. Matthew

VI

GROWING ISOLATION OF JESUS AND HIS MINISTRY

i

Now when John heard in the prison the works of the Christ, he sent by his disciples, and said unto him, Art thou he that cometh, or look we for another? And Jesus answered and said unto them, Go your way and tell John the things which ye do hear and see: the blind receive their sight, and the lame walk, the lepers are cleansed, and the deaf hear, and the dead are raised up, and the poor have good tidings preached to them. And blessed is he, whosoever shall find none occasion of stumbling in me. And as these went their way, Jesus began to say unto the multitudes concerning John: What went ye out into the wilderness to behold? a reed shaken with the wind? But what went ye out for to see? a man clothed in soft raiment? Behold, they that wear soft raiment are in kings' houses. But wherefore went ye out? to see a prophet? Yea, I say

Separation from John the Baptist

unto you, and much more than a prophet. This is he, of whom it is written, *Behold, I send my messenger before thy face, who shall prepare thy way before thee.* Verily I say unto you, Among them that are born of women there hath not arisen a greater than John the Baptist: yet he that is but little in the kingdom of heaven is greater than he. And from the days of John the Baptist until now the kingdom of heaven suffereth violence, and men of violence take it by force. For all the prophets and the law prophesied until John. And if ye are willing to receive it, this is Elijah, which is to come. He that hath ears to hear, let him hear. But whereunto shall I liken this generation? It is like unto children sitting in the marketplaces, which call unto their fellows, and say, We piped unto you, and ye did not dance; we wailed, and ye did not mourn. For John came neither eating nor drinking, and they say, He hath a devil. The Son of man came eating and drinking, and they say, Behold, a gluttonous man, and a winebibber, a friend of publicans and sinners! And wisdom is justified by her children.

ii

Then began he to upbraid the cities wherein most of his mighty works were done, because they repented not. Woe unto thee, Chorazin! woe unto thee, Bethsaida! for if the mighty works had been done in Tyre and Sidon which were done in you, they would have repented long ago in sackcloth and ashes. Howbeit I say unto you, it shall be more tolerable for Tyre and Sidon in the day of judgement than for you. And thou, Capernaum, shalt thou be exalted unto heaven? thou shalt go down unto Hades: for if the mighty works had been done in Sodom which were done in thee, it would have remained until this day. Howbeit I say unto you, that it shall be more tolerable for the land of Sodom in the day of judgement than for thee.

From the Wisdom of the World

At that season Jesus answered and said: I thank thee, O Father, Lord of heaven and earth, that thou didst hide these things from the wise and understanding, and didst reveal them unto babes: yea, Father, for so it was well-pleasing in thy sight. All things have been delivered unto me of my Father: and no one knoweth the Son, save the Father; neither doth any know the Father, save the Son, and he to whomsoever the Son willeth to reveal him. Come unto me, all ye that labour and are heavy laden, and I will give you rest. Take my yoke upon you, and learn of me; for I am meek and lowly in heart: and ye shall find rest unto your souls. For my yoke is easy, and my burden is light.

iii

At that season Jesus went on the sabbath day through the cornfields; and his disciples were an hungred, and began to pluck ears of corn, and to eat. But the Pharisees, when they saw it, said unto him, Behold, thy disciples do that which it is not lawful to do upon the sabbath.

<small>From the Pharisaic Doctrine of the Sabbath</small>
But he said unto them: **Have ye not read what David did, when he was an hungred, and they that were with him; how he entered into the house of God, and did eat the shewbread,** which it was not lawful for him to eat, neither for them that were with him, but only for the priests? Or have ye not read in the law, how that on the sabbath day the priests in the temple profane the sabbath, and are guiltless? But I say unto you, that one greater than the temple is here. But if ye had known what this meaneth, I desire mercy, and not sacrifice, ye would not have condemned the guiltless. For the Son of man is lord of the sabbath.

And he departed thence, and went into their synagogue: and behold, a man having a withered hand. And they asked him, saying, Is it lawful to heal on the sabbath day? that they might accuse him. And he said unto them: What man shall there be of you, that shall have one sheep, and if this fall into a pit on the sabbath day, will he not lay hold on it, and lift it out? How much then is a man of more value than a sheep! Wherefore it is lawful to do good on the sabbath day. Then saith he to the man, Stretch forth thy hand. And he stretched it forth; and it was restored whole, as the other.

But the Pharisees went out, and took counsel against him, how they might destroy him. And Jesus perceiving it withdrew from thence: and many followed him; and he healed them all, and charged them that they should not make him known: that it might be fulfilled which was spoken by Isaiah the prophet, saying, *Behold, my servant whom I have chosen; my beloved in whom my soul is well pleased: I will put my Spirit upon him, and he shall declare judgement to the Gentiles. He shall not strive, nor cry aloud; neither shall any one hear his voice in the streets; a bruised reed shall he not break, and smoking flax shall he not quench, till he send forth judgement unto victory: and in his name shall the Gentiles hope.*

iv

Then was brought unto him one possessed with a devil, blind and dumb: and he healed him, insomuch that the dumb man spake and saw. And all the multitudes were amazed, and said, Is this the son of David? But when the Pharisees heard it, they said, This man doth not cast out devils, but by Beelzebub the prince of the devils. And knowing their thoughts he said unto them: Every kingdom divided against itself is brought to desolation; and every city or house divided against itself shall not stand: and if Satan casteth out Satan, he is divided against himself; how then shall his kingdom stand? And if I by Beelzebub cast out devils, by whom do your sons cast them out? therefore shall they be

Pharisaic Blasphemy

your judges. But if I by the Spirit of God cast out devils, then is the kingdom of God come upon you. Or how can one enter into the house of the strong man, and spoil his goods, except he first bind the strong man? and then he will spoil his house. He that is not with me is against me; and he that gathereth not with me scattereth. Therefore I say unto you, Every sin and blasphemy shall be forgiven unto men; but the blasphemy against the Spirit shall not be forgiven. And whosoever shall speak a word against the Son of man, it shall be forgiven him; but whosoever shall speak against the Holy Spirit, it shall not be forgiven him, neither in this world, nor in that which is to come. Either make the tree good, and its fruit good; or make the tree corrupt, and its fruit corrupt: for the tree is known by its fruit. Ye offspring of vipers, how can ye, being evil, speak good things? for out of the abundance of the heart the mouth speaketh. The good man out of his good treasure bringeth forth good things: and the evil man out of his evil treasure bringeth forth evil things. And I say unto you, that every idle word that men shall speak, they shall give account thereof in the day of judgement. For by thy words thou shalt be justified, and by thy words thou shalt be condemned.

Then certain of the scribes and Pharisees answered him, saying, Master, we would see a sign from thee. But he answered and said unto them: **An evil and adulterous generation seeketh after a sign; and there shall no sign be**

St. Matthew   VI iv

given to it but the sign of Jonah the prophet.* The men of Nineveh shall stand up in the judgement with this generation, and shall condemn it: for they repented at the preaching of Jonah; and behold, a greater than Jonah is here. The queen of the south shall rise up in the judgement with this generation, and shall condemn it: for she came from the ends of the earth to hear the wisdom of Solomon; and behold, a greater than Solomon is here. But the unclean spirit, when he is gone out of the man, passeth through waterless places, seeking rest, and findeth it not. Then he saith, I will return into my house whence I came out; and when he is come, he findeth it empty, swept, and garnished. Then goeth he, and taketh with himself seven other spirits more evil than himself, and they enter in and dwell there: and the last state of that man becometh worse than the first. Even so shall it be also unto this evil generation.

While he was yet speaking to the multitudes, behold, his mother and his brethren stood without, seeking to speak to him. And one said unto him, Behold, thy mother and thy brethren stand without, seeking to speak to thee. But he answered and said unto him that told him, Who is my mother? and who are my brethren? And he stretched forth his hand towards his disciples, and said,

Separation from Mother and Brethren

---
* For as Jonah was three days and three nights in the belly of the whale, so shall the Son of man be three days and three nights in the heart of the earth.

VI iv   ↠ The Gospel

Behold, my mother and my brethren! For whosoever shall do the will of my Father which is in heaven, he is my brother, and sister, and mother.

VII

THE PUBLIC PARABLE AND THE PRIVATE INTERPRETATION

On that day went Jesus out of the house, and sat by the sea side. And there were gathered unto him great multitudes, so that he entered into a boat, and sat; and all the multitude stood on the beach. And he spake to them many things in parables, saying:

i

Behold, the sower went forth to sow; and as he sowed, some seeds fell by the way side, and the birds came and devoured them: and others fell upon the rocky places, where they had not much earth: and straightway they sprang up, because they had no deepness of earth: and when the sun was risen, they were scorched; and because they had no root, they withered away. And others fell upon the thorns; and the thorns grew up, and choked them: and others fell upon the good ground, and yielded fruit, some a hundredfold, some sixty, some thirty. He that hath ears, let him hear.

1. Parable of the Sower

VII i ⊶ The Gospel

And the disciples came, and said unto him, Why speakest thou unto them in parables? And he answered and said unto them: Unto you it is given to know the mysteries of the kingdom of heaven, but to them it is not given. For whosoever hath, to him shall be given, and he shall have abundance: but whosoever hath not, from him shall be taken away even that which he hath. Therefore speak I to them in parables; because seeing they see not, and hearing they hear not, neither do they understand. And unto them is fulfilled the prophecy of Isaiah, which saith: *By hearing ye shall hear, and shall in no wise understand; and seeing ye shall see, and shall in no wise perceive: for this people's heart is waxed gross, and their ears are dull of hearing, and their eyes they have closed; lest haply they should perceive with their eyes, and hear with their ears, and understand with their heart, and should turn again, and I should heal them.* But blessed are your eyes, for they see; and your ears, for they hear. For verily I say unto you, that many prophets and righteous men desired to see the things which ye see, and saw them not; and to hear the things which ye hear, and heard them not. Hear then ye the parable of the sower. When any one heareth the word of the kingdom, and understandeth it not, then cometh the evil one, and snatcheth away that which hath been sown in his heart. This is he that was sown by the way side. And he that was sown upon the rocky places, this is he that heareth the word, and straightway with joy receiveth it; yet hath he not root in himself, but endureth for a while; and when tribulation or persecution ariseth because of the word, straightway he stumbleth. And he that was sown among the thorns, this is he that heareth the word; and the care of the world, and the deceitfulness of riches, choke the word, and he becometh unfruitful. And he that was sown upon the good ground, this is he that heareth the word, and understandeth it; who verily beareth fruit, and bringeth forth, some a hundredfold, some sixty, some thirty.

ii

Another parable set he before them, saying: The kingdom of heaven is likened unto a man that sowed good seed in his field: but while men slept, his enemy came and sowed tares also among the wheat, and went away. *2. Parable of the Tares* But when the blade sprang up, and brought forth fruit, then appeared the tares also. And the servants of the householder came and said unto him, Sir, didst thou not sow good seed in thy field? whence then hath it tares? And he said unto them, An enemy hath done this. And the servants say unto him, Wilt thou then that we go and gather them up? But he saith, Nay; lest haply while ye gather up the tares, ye root up the wheat with them. Let both grow together until the harvest: and in the time of the harvest I will say to the reapers, Gather up first the tares, and bind them in bundles to burn them: but gather the wheat into my barn.

iii

Another parable set he before them, saying: **The kingdom of heaven is like unto a grain of mustard seed, which a man took, and sowed in his field: which indeed is less than all seeds; but when it is grown, it is greater than the herbs, and becometh a tree, so that the birds of the heaven come and lodge in the branches thereof.**

3. Parable of the Mustard Seed

iv

Another parable spake he unto them: **The kingdom of heaven is like unto leaven, which a woman took, and hid in three measures of meal, till it was all leavened.**

4. Of the Leaven

All these things spake Jesus in parables unto the multitudes; and without a parable spake he nothing unto them: that it might be fulfilled which was spoken by the prophet, saying,

I will open my mouth in parables;
I will utter things hidden from the foundation of the
  world.

Then he left the multitudes, and went into the house: and his disciples came unto him, saying, Explain unto us the parable of the tares of the field. And he answered and said: He that soweth the good seed is the Son of man; and the field is the world; and the good seed, these are the sons of the kingdom; and the tares are the sons of the evil one; and the enemy that sowed them is the devil: and the harvest is the end of the world; and the reapers are angels. As therefore the tares are gathered up and burned with fire; so shall it be in the end of the world. The Son of man shall send forth his angels, and they shall gather out of his kingdom all things that cause stumbling, and them that do iniquity, and shall cast them into the furnace of fire: there shall be the weeping and gnashing of teeth. Then shall the righteous shine forth as the sun in the kingdom of their Father. He that hath ears, let him hear.

v

The kingdom of heaven is like unto a treasure hidden in the field; which a man found, and hid; and in his joy he goeth and selleth all that he hath, and buyeth that field.

5. Parable of Treasure trove

vi

Again, the kingdom of heaven is like unto a man that is a merchant seeking goodly pearls: and having found one pearl of great price, he went and sold all that he had, and bought it.

6. Of the goodly Pearl

vii

Again, the kingdom of heaven is like unto a net, that was cast into the sea, and gathered of every kind: which, when it was filled, they drew up on the beach; and they sat down, and gathered the good into vessels, but the bad they cast away. So shall it be in the end of the world: the angels shall come forth, and sever the wicked from among the righteous, and shall cast them into the furnace of fire: there shall be the weeping and gnashing of teeth.

7. Of the Drag-net

Have ye understood all these things? They say unto him, Yea. And he said unto them: Therefore every scribe who hath been made a disciple to the kingdom of heaven is like unto a man that is a householder, which bringeth forth out of his treasure things new and old.

VIII

THE GREATER MIRACLES AND THE GROWING ANTAGONISM

i

And it came to pass, when Jesus had finished these parables, he departed thence. And coming into his own country he taught them in their synagogue, insomuch that they were astonished, and said, Whence hath this man this wisdom, and these mighty works? Is not this the carpenter's son? is not his mother called Mary? and his brethren, James, and Joseph, and Simon, and Judas? And his sisters, are they not all with us? Whence then hath this man all these things? And they were offended in him. But Jesus said unto them, A prophet is not without honour, save in his own country, and in his own house. And he did not many mighty works there because of their unbelief. *His own country offended*

ii

At that season Herod the tetrarch heard the report concerning Jesus, and said unto his servants, This is John the

Baptist; he is risen from the dead; and therefore do these powers work in him. For Herod had laid hold on John, and bound him, and put him in prison for the sake of Herodias, his brother Philip's wife; for John said unto him, It is not lawful for thee to have her. And when he would have put him to death, he feared the multitude, because they counted him as a prophet. But when Herod's birthday came, the daughter of Herodias danced in the midst, and pleased Herod; whereupon he promised with an oath to give her whatsoever she should ask. And she, being put forward by her mother, saith, Give me here in a charger the head of John the Baptist. And the king was grieved; but for the sake of his oaths, and of them which sat at meat with him, he commanded it to be given; and he sent, and beheaded John in the prison. And his head was brought in a charger, and given to the damsel: and she brought it to her mother. And his disciples came, and took up the corpse, and buried him; and they went and told Jesus.

Now when Jesus heard it, he withdrew from thence in a boat, to a desert place apart: and when the multitudes heard thereof, they followed him on foot from the cities. And he came forth, and saw a great multitude, and he had compassion on them, and healed their sick. And when even was come, the disciples came to him, saying, The place is desert, and the time is already past; send the multitudes away, that they may go into the villages, and

St. Matthew ✢ VIII ii

buy themselves food. But Jesus said unto them, They have no need to go away; give ye them to eat. And they say unto him, We have here but five loaves, and two fishes. And he said, Bring them hither to me. And he commanded the multitudes to sit down on the grass; and he took the five loaves, and the two fishes, and looking up to heaven, he blessed, and brake and gave the loaves to the disciples, and the disciples to the multitudes. And they did all eat, and were filled: and they took up that which remained over of the broken pieces, twelve baskets full. And they that did eat were about five thousand men, beside women and children. *A miracle of feeding*

And straightway he constrained the disciples to enter into the boat, and to go before him unto the other side, till he should send the multitudes away. And after he had sent the multitudes away, he went up into the mountain apart to pray: and when even was come, he was there alone. But the boat was now in the midst of the sea, distressed by the waves; for the wind was contrary. And in the fourth watch of the night he came unto them, walking upon the sea. And when the disciples saw him walking on the sea, they were troubled, saying, It is an apparition; and they cried out for fear. But straightway Jesus spake unto them, saying, Be of good cheer; it is I; be not afraid. And Peter answered him and said, Lord, if it be thou, *A miracle on the sea* bid me come unto thee upon the waters. And he said, Come. And Peter went down from the boat, and walked upon the waters, to come to Jesus. But when he saw the wind, he was afraid; and beginning to sink, he cried out, saying, Lord, save me. And immediately Jesus stretched forth his hand, and took hold of him, and saith unto him, O thou of little faith, wherefore didst thou doubt? And when they were gone up into the boat, the wind ceased. And they that were in the boat worshipped him, saying, Of a truth thou art the Son of God.

And when they had crossed over, they came to the land, unto Gennesaret. And when the men of that place knew him, they sent into all that region round about, and brought unto him all that were sick; and they besought him that they might only touch the border of his garment: and as many as touched were made whole.

iii

Then there come to Jesus from Jerusalem Pharisees and scribes, saying, Why do thy disciples transgress the Tradition of the Elders? for they wash not their hands when they eat bread. And he answered and said unto them: Why do ye also transgress the commandment of God because of your tradition? For God said, Honour thy father and thy mother: and, He that speaketh evil of father or mother, let him die the death. But ye say, Whosoever shall say to

Attack on the Tradition of the Elders

St. Matthew VIII iii

his father or his mother, That wherewith thou mightest have been profited by me is given to God; he shall not honour his father. And ye have made void the word of God because of your tradition. Ye hypocrites, well did Isaiah prophesy of you, saying: *This people honoureth me with their lips; but their heart is far from me. But in vain do they worship me, teaching as their doctrines the precepts of men.* And he called to him the multitude, and said unto them: Hear, and understand: Not that which entereth into the mouth defileth the man; but that which proceedeth out of the mouth, this defileth the man. Then came the disciples, and said unto him, Knowest thou that the Pharisees were offended, when they heard this saying? But he answered and said, Every plant which my heavenly Father planted not, shall be rooted up. Let them alone: they are blind guides. And if the blind guide the blind, both shall fall into a pit. And Peter answered and said unto him, Declare unto us the parable. And he said: Are ye also even yet without understanding? Perceive ye not, that whatsoever goeth into the mouth passeth into the belly, and is cast out into the draught? But the things which proceed out of the mouth come forth out of the heart; and they defile the man. For out of the heart come forth evil thoughts, murders, adulteries, fornications, thefts, false witness, railings: these are the things which defile the man: but to eat with unwashen hands defileth not the man.

iv

And Jesus went out thence, and withdrew into the parts of Tyre and Sidon. And behold, a Canaanitish woman came out from those borders, and cried, saying, Have mercy on me, O Lord, thou son of David; my daughter is grievously vexed with a devil. But he answered her not a word. And his disciples came and besought him, saying, Send her away; for she crieth after us. But he answered and said, I was not sent but unto the lost sheep of the house of Israel. But she came and worshipped him, saying, Lord, help me. And he answered and said, It is not meet to take the children's bread and cast it to the dogs. But she said, Yea, Lord: for even the dogs eat of the crumbs which fall from their masters' table. Then Jesus answered and said unto her, O woman, great is thy faith: be it done unto thee even as thou wilt. And her daughter was healed from that hour.

v

And Jesus departed thence, and came nigh unto the sea of Galilee; and he went up into the mountain, and sat there. And there came unto him great multitudes, having with them the lame, blind, dumb, maimed, and many others, and they cast them down at his feet; and he healed them: insomuch that the multitude wondered, when they saw the dumb speaking, the maimed whole, and the lame walking, and the blind seeing: and they glorified the God of Israel.

And Jesus called unto him his disciples, and said, I have compassion on the multitude, because they continue with me now three days and have nothing to eat: and I would not send them away fasting, lest haply they faint in the way. And the disciples say unto him, Whence should we have so many loaves in a desert place, as to fill so great a multitude? And Jesus saith unto them, How many loaves have ye? And they said, Seven, and a few small fishes. And he commanded the multitude to sit down on the ground; and he took the seven loaves and the fishes; and he gave thanks and brake, and gave to the disciples, and the disciples to the multitudes. And they did all eat, and were filled: and they took up that which remained over of the broken pieces, seven baskets full. And they that did eat were four thousand men, beside women and children. And he sent away the multitudes, and entered into the boat, and came into the borders of Magadan.

A miraculous feeding and

And the Pharisees and Sadducees came, and tempting him asked him to shew them a sign from heaven. But he answered and said unto them: When it is evening, ye say, It will be fair weather: for the heaven is red. And in the morning, It will be foul weather today: for the heaven is red and

the Pharisaic 'Leaven'

lowring. Ye know how to discern the face of the heaven; but ye cannot discern the signs of the times. An evil and adulterous generation seeketh after a sign; and there shall no sign be given unto it, but the sign of Jonah. And he left them, and departed.

And the disciples came to the other side and forgot to take bread. And Jesus said unto them, Take heed and beware of the leaven of the Pharisees and Sadducees. And they reasoned among themselves, saying, We took no bread. And Jesus perceiving it said: O ye of little faith, why reason ye among yourselves, because ye have no bread? Do ye not yet perceive, neither remember the five loaves of the five thousand, and how many baskets ye took up? Neither the seven loaves of the four thousand, and how many baskets ye took up? How is it that ye do not perceive that I spake not to you concerning bread? But beware of the leaven of the Pharisees and Sadducees. Then understood they how that he bade them not beware of the leaven of bread, but of the teaching of the Pharisees and Sadducees.

St. Matthew

IX

FULLER RECOGNITION BY THE DISCIPLES OF THE KINGDOM AND QUESTIONS ARISING THEREUPON

i

Now when Jesus came into the parts of Cæsarea Philippi, he asked his disciples, saying, Who do men say that the Son of man is? And they said, Some say John the Baptist; some, Elijah: and others, Jeremiah, or one of the prophets. He saith unto them, But who say ye that I am? And Simon Peter answered and said, Thou art the Christ, the Son of the living God. And Jesus answered and said unto him: Blessed art thou, Simon Bar-Jonah: for flesh and blood hath not revealed it unto thee, but my Father which is in heaven. And I also say unto thee, that thou art 'Peter,' and upon this 'rock' I will build my church; and the gates of Hades shall not prevail against it. I will give unto thee the keys of the kingdom of heaven: and whatsoever thou shalt bind on earth shall be bound in heaven: and what-

Recognition of the Christ

IX i   The Gospel

soever thou shalt loose on earth shall be loosed in heaven. Then charged he the disciples that they should tell no man that he was the Christ.

From that time began Jesus to shew unto his disciples, how that he must go unto Jerusalem, and suffer many *and Revelation of his Sufferings* things of the elders and chief priests and scribes, and be killed, and the third day be raised up. And Peter took him, and began to rebuke him, saying, Be it far from thee, Lord: this shall never be unto thee. But he turned, and said unto Peter, Get thee behind me, Satan: thou art a stumblingblock unto me: for thou mindest not the things of God, but the things of men. Then said Jesus unto his disciples: **If any man would come after me, let him deny himself, and take up his cross, and follow me. For whosoever would save his life, shall lose it: and whosoever shall lose his life for my sake shall find it. For what shall a man be profited, if he shall gain the whole world, and forfeit his life? or what shall a man give in exchange for his life? For the Son of man shall come in the glory of his Father with his angels; and then shall he render unto every man according to his deeds. Verily I say unto you, There be some of them that stand here, which shall in no wise taste of death, till they see the Son of man coming in his kingdom.**

And after six days Jesus taketh with him Peter, and James, and John his brother, and bringeth them up into a high mountain apart: and he was transfigured before them: and his face did shine as the sun, and his garments became white as the light. And behold, there appeared unto them Moses and Elijah talking with him. And Peter answered, and said unto Jesus, Lord, it is good for us to be here: if thou wilt, I will make here three tabernacles; one for thee, and one for Moses, and one for Elijah. While he was yet speaking, behold, a bright cloud overshadowed them: and behold, a voice out of the cloud, saying, This is my beloved Son, in whom I am well pleased; hear ye him. And when the disciples heard it, they fell on their face, and were sore afraid. And Jesus came and touched them and said, Arise, and be not afraid. And lifting up their eyes, they saw no one, save Jesus only. *The Transfiguration*

And as they were coming down from the mountain, Jesus commanded them, saying, Tell the vision to no man, until the Son of man be risen from the dead. And his disciples asked him, saying, Why then say the scribes that Elijah must first come? And he answered and said: Elijah indeed cometh, and shall restore all things: but I say unto you, that Elijah is come already, and they knew him not, but did unto him whatsoever they listed. Even so shall the Son of man also suffer of them. Then understood the disciples that he spake unto them of John the Baptist. *Question of Elijah's coming*

And when they were come to the multitude, there came

to him a man, kneeling to him, and saying, Lord, have mercy on my son: for he is epileptic, and suffereth grievously: for oft-times he falleth into the fire, and oft-times into the water. And I brought him to thy disciples, and they could not cure him. And Jesus answered and said, O faithless and perverse generation, how long shall I be with you? how long shall I bear with you? bring him hither to me. And Jesus rebuked him; and the devil went out from him: and the boy was cured from that hour. Then came the disciples to Jesus apart, and said, Why could not we cast it out? And he saith unto them, Because of your little faith. **For verily I say unto you, If ye have faith as a grain of mustard seed, ye shall say unto this mountain, Remove hence to yonder place; and it shall remove; and nothing shall be impossible unto you.**

ii

And while they abode in Galilee, Jesus said unto them, The Son of man shall be delivered up into the hands of men; and they shall kill him, and the third day he shall be raised up. And they were exceeding sorry.

And when they were come to Capernaum, they that received the half-shekel came to Peter, and said, Doth not your master pay the half-shekel? He saith, Yea. And when he came into the house, Jesus spake first to him, saying, What thinkest thou, Simon? the kings of the earth,

St. Matthew ❧ IX ii

from whom do they receive toll or tribute? from their sons, or from strangers? And when he said, From strangers, Jesus said unto him, Therefore the sons are free. But, lest we cause them to stumble, go thou to the sea, and cast a hook, and take up the fish that first cometh up; and when thou hast opened his mouth, thou shalt find a shekel: that take, and give unto them for me and thee.

Do sons of the kingdom pay toll?

In that hour came the disciples unto Jesus, saying, Who then is greatest in the kingdom of heaven? And he called to him a little child, and set him in the midst of them, and said: **Verily I say unto you, Except ye turn, and become as little children, ye shall in no wise enter into the kingdom of heaven. Whosoever therefore shall humble himself as this little child, the same is the greatest in the kingdom of heaven. And whoso shall receive one such little child in my name receiveth me:** but whoso shall cause one of these little ones which believe on me to stumble, it is profitable for him that a great millstone should be hanged about his neck, and that he should be sunk in the depth of the sea. Woe unto the world because of occasions of stumbling! for it must needs be that the occasions come; but woe to that man through whom the occasion cometh! And if thy hand or thy foot causeth thee to stumble, cut it off, and cast it from thee: it is good for thee to enter into life maimed or halt, rather than having two hands or two feet

Greatness in the kingdom of heaven

to be cast into the eternal fire. And if thine eye causeth thee to stumble, pluck it out, and cast it from thee: it is good for thee to enter into life with one eye, rather than having two eyes to be cast into the hell of fire. See that ye despise not one of these little ones; for I say unto you, that in heaven their angels do always behold the face of my Father which is in heaven. How think ye? if any man have a hundred sheep, and one of them be gone astray, doth he not leave the ninety and nine, and go unto the mountains, and seek that which goeth astray? And if so be that he find it, verily I say unto you, he rejoiceth over it more than over the ninety and nine which have not gone astray. Even so it is not the will of your Father which is in heaven, that one of these little ones should perish.

And if thy brother sin against thee, go, shew him his fault between thee and him alone: if he hear thee, thou *Treatment of sin in the new kingdom* hast gained thy brother. But if he hear thee not, take with thee one or two more, that at the mouth of two witnesses or three every word may be established. And if he refuse to hear them, tell it unto the church: and if he refuse to hear the church also, let him be unto thee as the Gentile and the publican. Verily I say unto you, What things soever ye shall bind on earth shall be bound in heaven: and what things soever ye shall loose on earth shall be loosed in heaven. Again I say unto you, that if two of you shall agree on earth as touching anything that they shall ask, it shall be done for them of my Father which is in heaven. For where two or three are gathered together in my name, there am I in the midst of them.

Then came Peter, and said to him, Lord, how oft shall my brother sin against me, and I forgive him? until seven times? Jesus saith unto him, I say not unto thee, Until seven times; but, Until seventy times and seven. Therefore is the kingdom of heaven likened unto a certain king, which would make a reckoning with his servants. And when he had begun to reckon, one was brought unto him, which owed him ten thousand talents. But forasmuch as he had not wherewith to pay, his lord commanded him to be sold, and his wife, and children, and all that he had, and payment to be made. *Parable of the Fellow Servants* The servant therefore fell down and worshipped him, saying, Lord, have patience with me, and I will pay thee all. And the lord of that servant, being moved with compassion, released him, and forgave him the debt. But that servant went out, and found one of his fellow-servants, which owed him a hundred pence: and he laid hold on him, and took him by the throat, saying, Pay what thou owest. So his fellow-servant fell down and besought him, saying, Have patience with me, and I will pay thee. And he would not: but went and cast him into prison, till he should pay that which was due. So when his fellow-servants saw what was done, they were exceeding sorry, and came and told unto their lord all that was done. Then his lord called him unto him, and saith to him, Thou wicked servant, I forgave thee all that debt, because thou besoughtest me: shouldest not thou also have had mercy on thy fellow-servant, even as I had mercy on thee? And his lord was wroth, and delivered him to the tormentors, till he should pay all that was due. So shall also my heavenly Father do unto you, if ye forgive not every one his brother from your hearts.

iii

And it came to pass when Jesus had finished these words, he departed from Galilee, and came into the borders of Judæa beyond Jordan; and great multitudes followed him; and he healed them there.

And there came unto him Pharisees, tempting him, and saying, Is it lawful for a man to put away his wife for every cause? And he answered and said: **Have ye not read, that he which made them from the beginning made them male and female, and said, For this cause shall a man leave his father and mother, and shall cleave to his wife; and the twain shall become one flesh? So that they are no more twain, but one flesh. What therefore God hath joined together, let not man put asunder.** They say unto him, Why then did Moses command to give a bill of divorcement, and

Question of Divorce and Marriage

to put her away? He saith unto them: **Moses for your hardness of heart suffered you to put away your wives: but from the beginning it hath not been so.** And I say unto you, Whosoever shall put away his wife, except for fornication, and shall marry another, committeth adultery: and he that marrieth her when she is put away committeth adultery. The disciples say unto him, If the case of the man is so with his wife, it is not expedient to marry. But he said unto them: **All men cannot receive this saying, but they to whom it is given.** For there are eunuchs, which were so born from their mother's womb: and there are eunuchs, which were made eunuchs by men: and there are eunuchs, which made themselves eunuchs for the kingdom of heaven's sake. **He that is able to receive it, let him receive it.**

Then were there brought unto him little children, that he should lay his hands on them, and pray: and the disciples rebuked them. But Jesus said, Suffer the little children, and forbid them not, to come unto me: for of such is the kingdom of heaven. And he laid his hands on them, and departed thence.

And behold, one came to him and said, Master, what good thing shall I do, that I may have eternal life? And he said unto him, Why askest thou me concerning that which is good? One there is who is good: but if thou wouldest enter into life, keep the commandments. He saith unto him, Which? And Jesus said, Thou shalt not kill, Thou shalt not commit adultery, Thou shalt not steal, Thou shalt not bear false witness, Honour thy father and thy mother: and, Thou shalt love thy neighbour as thyself. The young man saith unto him, All these things have I observed: what lack I yet? Jesus said unto him, <small>Mammon and the kingdom of heaven</small> If thou wouldest be perfect, go, sell that thou hast, and give to the poor, and thou shalt have treasure in heaven: and come, follow me. But when the young man heard the saying, he went away sorrowful: for he was one that had great possessions.

And Jesus said unto his disciples: **Verily I say unto you, It is hard for a rich man to enter into the kingdom of heaven. And again I say unto you, It is easier for a camel to go through a needle's eye, than for a rich man to enter into the kingdom of God.** And when the disciples heard it, they were astonished exceedingly, saying, Who then can be saved? And Jesus looking upon them said to them, **With men this is impossible; but with God all things are possible.** Then answered Peter and said unto him, Lo, we have left all, and followed thee; what then shall we have? And Jesus said unto them: **Verily I say unto you, that ye which have followed me, in the regeneration when the Son of man shall sit on the throne of his glory, ye also shall sit upon twelve thrones, judging the twelve tribes of Israel. And every one that hath left houses, or brethren, or sisters, or father, or mother, or children, or lands, for my name's sake, shall receive a**

St. Matthew   IX iii

hundredfold, and shall inherit eternal life. But many shall be last that are first; and first that are last. For the kingdom of heaven is like unto a man that is a householder, which went out early in the morning to hire labourers into his vineyard. And when he had agreed with the labourers for a penny a day, he sent them into his vineyard. And he went out about the third hour, and saw others standing in the marketplace idle; and to them he said, Go ye also into the vineyard, and whatsoever is right I will give you. And they went their way. Again he went out about the sixth and the ninth hour, and did likewise. And about the eleventh hour he went out, and found others standing; and he saith unto them, Why stand ye here all the day idle? They say unto him, Because no man hath hired us. He saith unto them, Go ye also into the vineyard. And when even was come, the lord of the vineyard saith unto his steward, Call the labourers, and pay them their hire, beginning from the last unto the first. And when they came that were hired about the eleventh hour, they received every man a penny. And when the first came, they supposed that they would receive more; and they likewise received every man a penny. And when they received it, they murmured against the householder, saying, These last have spent but one hour, and thou hast made them equal unto us, which have borne the burden of the day and the scorching heat. But he answered and said

Parable of the Hired Labourers

to one of them, Friend, I do thee no wrong: didst not thou agree with me for a penny? Take up that which is thine, and go thy way; it is my will to give unto this last, even as unto thee. Is it not lawful for me to do what I will with mine own? or is thine eye evil, because I am good? So the last shall be first, and the first last.

iv

And as Jesus was going up to Jerusalem, he took the twelve disciples apart, and in the way he said unto them, Behold, we go up to Jerusalem; and the Son of man shall be delivered unto the chief priests and scribes; and they shall condemn him to death, and shall deliver him unto the Gentiles to mock, and to scourge, and to crucify: and the third day he shall be raised up.

Then came to him the mother of the sons of Zebedee with her sons, worshipping him, and asking a certain thing of him. And he said unto her, What wouldest thou? She saith unto him, Command that these my two sons may sit, one on thy right hand, and one on thy left hand, in thy kingdom. But Jesus answered and said, Ye know not what ye ask. Are ye able to drink the cup that I am about to drink? They say unto him, We are able. He saith unto them, My cup indeed ye shall drink: but to sit on my right hand, and on my left hand, is not mine to give, but it is for them for whom it hath been prepared of my Father. And when the ten heard it, they were moved with indignation concerning the two brethren. But Jesus called them unto him, and said: Ye know that the rulers of the Gentiles lord it over them, and their great ones exercise authority over them. Not so shall it be among you: but whosoever would become great among you shall be your minister; and whosoever would be first among you shall be your servant: even as the Son of man came not to be ministered unto, but to minister, and to give his life a ransom for many.

Lordship in the kingdom is service

And as they went out from Jericho, a great multitude followed him. And behold, two blind men sitting by the way side, when they heard that Jesus was passing by, cried out, saying, Lord, have mercy on us, thou son of David. And the multitude rebuked them, that they should hold their peace: but they cried out the more, saying, Lord, have mercy on us, thou son of David. And Jesus stood still, and called them, and said, What will ye that I should do unto you? They say unto him, Lord, that our eyes may be opened. And Jesus, being moved with compassion, touched their eyes: and straightway they received their sight, and followed him.

X

ENTRY INTO JERUSALEM AND FINAL BREACH WITH THE RULING CLASSES

i

Royal Entry into Jerusalem
And when they drew nigh unto Jerusalem, and came unto Bethphage, unto the mount of Olives, then Jesus sent two disciples, saying unto them, Go into the village that is over against you, and straightway ye shall find an ass tied, and a colt with her: loose them, and bring them unto me. And if any one say aught unto you, ye shall say, The Lord hath need of them; and straightway he will send them. Now this is come to pass, that it might be fulfilled which was spoken by the prophet, saying:

> *Tell ye the daughter of Zion,*
> *Behold, thy King cometh unto thee,*
> *Meek, and riding upon an ass,*
> *And upon a colt the foal of an ass.*

And the disciples went, and did even as Jesus appointed them, and brought the ass, and the colt, and put on them their garments; and he sat thereon. And the most part of the multitude spread their garments in the way; and others cut branches from the trees, and spread them in the way. And the multitudes that went before him, and that followed, cried, saying, 'Hosanna to the son of David'— 'Blessed is he that cometh in the name of the Lord'— 'Hosanna in the highest.' And when he was come into Jerusalem, all the city was stirred, saying, Who is this? And the multitudes said, This is the prophet, Jesus, from Nazareth of Galilee.

And Jesus entered into the temple of God, and cast out all them that sold and bought in the temple, and overthrew the tables of the money-changers, and the seats of them that sold the doves; and he saith unto them, It is written, My house shall be called a house of prayer; but ye make it a den of robbers. And the blind and the lame came to him in the temple: and he healed them. But when the chief priests and the scribes saw the wonderful things that he did, and the children that were crying in the temple and saying, 'Hosanna to the son of David'; they were moved with indignation, and said unto him, Hearest thou what these are saying? And Jesus saith unto them, Yea: did ye never read, *Out of the mouth of babes and sucklings thou hast perfected praise?* And he left them, and went forth out of the city to Bethany, and lodged there.

Now in the morning as he returned to the city, he hun-

[margin: Cleansing of the Temple]

gered. And seeing a fig tree by the way side, he came to it, and found nothing thereon, but leaves only; and he saith unto it, Let there be no fruit from thee henceforward for ever. And immediately the fig tree withered away. And when the disciples saw it, they marvelled, saying, How did the fig tree immediately wither away? And Jesus answered and said unto them: **Verily I say unto you, If ye have faith, and doubt not, ye shall not only do what is done to the fig tree, but even if ye shall say unto this mountain, Be thou taken up and cast into the sea, it shall be done. And all things, whatsoever ye shall ask in prayer, believing, ye shall receive.**

Incident of the Fig Tree

ii

And when he was come into the temple, the chief priests and the elders of the people came unto him as he was teaching, and said, By what authority doest thou these things? and who gave thee this authority? And Jesus answered and said unto them, I also will ask you one question, which if ye tell me, I likewise will tell you by what authority I do these things. The baptism of John, whence was it? from heaven or from men? And they reasoned with themselves, saying, If we shall say, From heaven; he will say unto us, Why then did ye not believe him? But if we shall say, From men; we fear the multitude; for all hold

The Authority of Jesus challenged

St. Matthew

John as a prophet. And they answered Jesus, and said, We know not. He also said unto them, Neither tell I you by what authority I do these things.

But what think ye? A man had two sons; and he came to the first, and said, Son, go work today in the vineyard. And he answered and said, I will not: but afterward he repented himself, and went. And he came to the second, and said likewise. And he answered and said, I go, sir: and went not. Whether of the twain did the will of his father? They say, the first. Jesus saith unto them: **Verily I say unto you, that the publicans and the harlots go into the kingdom of God before you.** For John came unto you in the way of righteousness, and ye believed him not: but the publicans and the harlots believed him: and ye, when ye saw it, did not even repent yourselves afterward, that ye might believe him. *Parable of the Two Sons*

Hear another parable: There was a man that was a householder, which planted a vineyard, and set a hedge about it, and digged a winepress in it, and built a tower, and let it out to husbandmen, and went into another country. And when the season of the fruits drew near, he sent his servants to the husbandmen, to receive his fruits. And the husbandmen took his servants, and beat one, and killed another, and stoned another. Again, he sent other servants more than the first: and they did unto *Parable of the Husbandmen and the Heir* them in like manner. But afterward he sent unto them his son, saying, They will reverence my son. But the husbandmen, when they saw the son, said among themselves, This is the heir; come, let us kill him, and take his inheritance. And they took him, and cast him forth out of the vineyard, and killed him. When therefore the lord of the vineyard shall come, what will he do unto those husbandmen? They say unto him, He will miserably destroy those miserable men, and will let out the vineyard unto other husbandmen, which shall render him the fruits in their seasons. Jesus saith unto them, Did ye never read in the scriptures,

> *The stone which the builders rejected,*
> *The same was made the head of the corner:*
> *This was from the Lord,*
> *And it is marvellous in our eyes?*

Therefore say I unto you, The kingdom of God shall be taken away from you, and shall be given to a nation bringing forth the fruits thereof. And he that falleth on this stone shall be broken to pieces: but on whomsoever it shall fall, it will scatter him as dust.

And when the chief priests and the Pharisees heard his parables, they perceived that he spake of them. And when they sought to lay hold on him, they feared the multitudes, because they took him for a prophet.

And Jesus answered and spake again in parables unto

them, saying: The kingdom of heaven is likened unto a certain king, which made a marriage feast for his son, and sent forth his servants to call them that were bidden to the marriage feast: and they would not come. Again he sent forth other servants, saying, Tell them that are bidden, Behold, I have made ready my dinner: my oxen and my fatlings are killed, and all things are ready: come to the marriage feast. But they made light of it, and went their ways, one to his own farm, another to his merchandise: and the rest laid hold on his servants, and entreated them shamefully, and killed them. But the king was wroth; and he sent his armies, and destroyed those murderers, and burned their city. Then saith he to his servants, The wedding is ready, but they that were bidden were not worthy. Go ye therefore unto the partings of the highways, and as many as ye shall find, bid to the marriage feast. And those servants went out into the highways, and gathered together all as many as they found, both bad and good: and the wedding was filled with guests. But when the king came in to behold the guests, he saw there a man which had not on a wedding-garment: and he saith unto him, Friend, how camest thou in hither not having a wedding-garment? And he was speechless. Then the king said to the servants, Bind him hand and foot, and cast him out into the outer darkness; there shall be the weeping and gnashing of teeth. For many are called, but few chosen.

Parable of the Marriage Feast

iii

Then went the Pharisees, and took counsel how they might ensnare him in his talk. And they send to him their disciples, with the Herodians, saying, Master, we know that thou art true, and teachest the way of God in truth, and carest not for any one: for thou regardest not the person of men. Tell us therefore, What thinkest thou? Is it lawful to give tribute unto Cæsar, or not? But Jesus perceived their wickedness, and said, Why tempt ye me, ye hypocrites? Shew me the tribute money. And they brought unto him a penny. And he saith unto them, Whose is this image and superscription? They say unto him, Cæsar's. Then saith he unto them, **Render therefore unto Cæsar the things that are Cæsar's; and unto God the things that are God's.** And when they heard it, they marvelled, and left him, and went their way.

<small>Questions proposed as snares</small>

On that day there came to him Sadducees, which say that there is no resurrection: and they asked him, saying, Master, Moses said, If a man die, having no children, his brother shall marry his wife, and raise up seed unto his brother. Now there were with us seven brethren: and the first married and deceased, and having no seed left his wife unto his brother; in like manner the second also, and the third, unto the seventh. And after them all the woman died. In the resurrection therefore whose wife shall she be of the seven? for they all had her. But Jesus answered and said unto them: **Ye do err, not knowing the scriptures, nor the power of God.** For in the resurrection they neither marry, nor are given in marriage, but are as angels in heaven. But as touching the resurrection of the dead, have ye not read that which was spoken unto you by God, saying, **I am the God of Abraham, and the God of Isaac, and the God of Jacob?** God is not the God of the dead, but of the living. And when the multitudes heard it, they were astonished at his teaching.

But the Pharisees, when they heard that he had put the Sadducees to silence, gathered themselves together. And one of them, a lawyer, asked him a question, tempting him, Master, which is the great commandment in the law? And he said unto him: **Thou shalt love the Lord thy God with all thy heart, and with all thy soul, and with all thy mind. This is the great and first commandment. And a second like unto it is this, Thou shalt love thy neighbour as thyself. On these two commandments hangeth the whole law, and the prophets.**

Now while the Pharisees were gathered together, Jesus asked them a question, saying, What think ye of the Christ? whose son is he? They say unto him, The son of David. He saith unto them, How then doth David in the Spirit call him Lord, saying,

The Lord said unto my Lord,
Sit thou on my right hand,
Till I put thine enemies underneath thy feet?

If David then calleth him Lord, how is he his son? And no one was able to answer him a word, neither durst any man from that day forth ask him any more questions.

iv

Then spake Jesus to the multitudes and to his disciples, saying: The scribes and the Pharisees sit on Moses' seat: all things therefore whatsoever they bid you, these do and observe: but do not ye after their works; for they say, and do not. Yea, they bind heavy burdens and grievous to be borne, and lay them on men's shoulders; but they themselves will not move them with their finger. But all their works they do for to be seen of men: for they make broad their phylacteries, and enlarge the borders of their garments, and love the chief place at feasts, and the chief seats in the synagogues, and the salutations in the marketplaces, and to be called of men, Rabbi. But be not ye called Rabbi: for one is your teacher, and all ye are brethren. And call no man your father on the earth: for one is your Father, which is in heaven. Neither be ye called masters: for one is your master, even the Christ. But he that is greatest among you shall be your servant.

And whosoever shall exalt himself shall be humbled; and whosoever shall humble himself shall be exalted.

1

But woe unto you, scribes and Pharisees, hypocrites! because ye shut the kingdom of heaven against men: for ye enter not in yourselves, neither suffer ye them that are entering in to enter.

2

Woe unto you, scribes and Pharisees, hypocrites! for ye compass sea and land to make one proselyte; and when he is become so, ye make him twofold more a son of hell than yourselves.

3

Woe unto you, ye blind guides, which say, Whosoever shall swear by the temple, it is nothing; but whosoever shall swear by the gold of the temple, he is a debtor. Ye fools and blind: for whether is greater, the gold, or the temple that hath sanctified the gold? And, Whosoever shall swear by the altar, it is nothing; but whosoever shall swear by the gift that is upon it, he is a debtor. Ye blind: for whether is greater, the gift, or the altar that sanctifieth the gift? He therefore that sweareth by the altar, sweareth by it, and by all things thereon. And he that sweareth by the temple, sweareth by it, and by him that dwelleth therein. And he that sweareth by the heaven, sweareth by the throne of God, and by him that sitteth thereon.

4

Woe unto you, scribes and Pharisees, hypocrites! for ye tithe mint and anise and cummin, and have left undone the weightier matters of the law, judgement, and mercy, and faith: but these ye ought to have done, and not to have left the other undone. Ye blind guides, which strain out the gnat, and swallow the camel.

5

Woe unto you, scribes and Pharisees, hypocrites! for ye cleanse the outside of the cup and of the platter, but within they are full from extortion and excess. Thou blind Pharisee, cleanse first the inside of the cup and of the platter, that the outside thereof may become clean also.

6

Woe unto you, scribes and Pharisees, hypocrites! for ye are like unto whited sepulchres, which outwardly appear beautiful, but inwardly are full of dead men's bones, and of all uncleanness. Even so ye also outwardly appear righteous unto men, but inwardly ye are full of hypocrisy and iniquity.

7

Woe unto you, scribes and Pharisees, hypocrites! for ye build the sepulchres of the prophets, and garnish the tombs of the righteous, and say, If we had been in the days of our fathers, we should not have been partakers with them in the blood of the prophets. Wherefore ye witness to yourselves, that ye are sons of them that slew the prophets. Fill ye up then the measure of your fathers. Ye serpents, ye offspring of vipers, how shall ye escape the judgement of hell? " Therefore, behold, I send unto you prophets, and wise men, and scribes: some of them shall ye kill and crucify; and some of them shall ye scourge in your synagogues, and persecute from city to city: that upon you may come all the righteous blood shed on the earth, from the blood of Abel the righteous unto the blood of Zachariah son of Barachiah, whom ye slew between the sanctuary and the altar." Verily I say unto you, All these things shall come upon this generation.

O Jerusalem, Jerusalem, which killeth the prophets, and stoneth them that are sent unto her! how often would I have gathered thy children together, even as a hen gathereth her chickens under her wings, and ye would not! Behold, your house is left unto you desolate. For I say unto you, Ye shall not see me henceforth, till ye shall say, Blessed is he that cometh in the name of the Lord.

XI

DISCOURSE TO THE DISCIPLES: THE SEVEN-FOLD REVELATION OF THE END

And Jesus went out from the temple, and was going on his way; and his disciples came to him to shew him the buildings of the temple. But he answered and said unto them, See ye not all these things? verily I say unto you, There shall not be left here one stone upon another, that shall not be thrown down.

And as he sat on the mount of Olives, the disciples came unto him privately, saying, Tell us, when shall these things be? and what shall be the sign of thy coming, and of the end of the world? And Jesus answered and said unto them:

1. Take heed that no man lead you astray. For many shall come in my name, saying, I am the Christ; and shall lead many astray. And ye shall hear of wars and rumours of wars: see that ye be not troubled: for these things must needs come to pass; but the end is not yet. For nation

shall rise against nation, and kingdom against kingdom: and there shall be famines and earthquakes in divers places. But all these things are the beginning of travail. Then shall they deliver you up unto tribulation, and shall kill you: and ye shall be hated of all the nations for my name's sake. And then shall many stumble, and shall deliver up one another, and shall hate one another. And many false prophets shall arise, and shall lead many astray. And because iniquity shall be multiplied, the love of the many shall wax cold. But he that endureth to the end, the same shall be saved. And this gospel of the kingdom shall be preached in the whole world for a testimony unto all the nations; and then shall the end come. *Every tribulation is not the end*

2. When therefore ye see the abomination of desolation, which was spoken of by Daniel the prophet, standing in the holy place (let him that readeth understand), then let them that are in Judæa flee unto the mountains: let him that is on the housetop not go down to take out the things that are in his house: and let him that is in the field not return back to take his cloke. But woe unto them that are with child and to them that give suck in those days! And pray ye that your flight be not in the winter, neither on a sabbath: for then shall be great tribulation, such as hath not been from the beginning of the world until now, no, nor ever shall be. And except those days had been short- *The tribulation of Judæa*

ened, no flesh would have been saved: but for the elect's sake those days shall be shortened. Then if any man shall say unto you, Lo, here is the Christ, or, Here; believe it not. For there shall arise false Christs, and false prophets, and shall shew great signs and wonders; so as to lead astray, if possible, even the elect. Behold, I have told you beforehand. If therefore they shall say unto you, Behold, he is in the wilderness; go not forth: Behold, he is in the inner chambers; believe it not. For as the lightning cometh forth from the east, and is seen even unto the west; so shall be the coming of the Son of man. Wheresoever the carcase is, there will the eagles be gathered together.

3. But immediately, after the tribulation of those days, the sun shall be darkened, and the moon shall not give her light, and the stars shall fall from heaven, and the powers of the heavens shall be shaken: and then shall appear the sign of the Son of man in heaven: and then shall all the

The tribulation of the Coming of the Son of Man — tribes of the earth mourn, and they shall see the Son of man coming on the clouds of heaven with power and great glory. And he shall send forth his angels with a great sound of a trumpet, and they shall gather together his elect from the four winds, from one end of heaven to the other.

4. Now from the fig tree learn her parable: when her branch is now become tender, and putteth forth its leaves, ye know that the summer is nigh; even so ye also, when ye

St. Matthew XI

see all these things, know ye that it is nigh, even at the doors. Verily I say unto you, This generation shall not pass away, till all these things be accomplished. Heaven and earth shall pass away, but my words shall not pass away. But of that day and hour knoweth no one, not even the angels of heaven, neither the Son, but the Father only. And as were the days of Noah, so shall be the coming of the Son of man. For as in those days which were before the flood they were eating and drinking, marrying and giving in marriage, until the day that Noah entered into the ark, and they knew not until the flood came, and took them all away; so shall be the coming of the Son of man. Then shall two men be in the field; one is taken, and one is left: two women shall be grinding at the mill; one is taken, and one is left. *The one foreshadowed by tokens, the other will come suddenly*

5. Watch therefore: for ye know not on what day your Lord cometh. But know this, that if the master of the house had known in what watch the thief was coming, he would have watched, and would not have suffered his house to be broken through. Therefore be ye also ready: for in an hour that ye think not the Son of man cometh. Who then is the faithful and wise servant, whom his lord hath set over his household, to give them their food in due season? Blessed is that servant, whom his lord when he cometh shall find so doing: verily I say unto you, that he will set him *The Moral is Watchfulness.*

over all that he hath. But if that evil servant shall say in his heart, My lord tarrieth; and shall begin to beat his fellow-servants, and shall eat and drink with the drunken; the lord of that servant shall come in a day when he expecteth not, and in an hour when he knoweth not, and shall cut him asunder, and appoint his portion with the hypocrites: there shall be the weeping and gnashing of teeth.

Then shall the kingdom of heaven be likened unto ten virgins, which took their lamps, and went forth to meet the bridegroom. And five of them were foolish, and five were wise. For the foolish, when they took their lamps, took no oil with them: but the wise took oil in their vessels with their lamps. Now while the bridegroom tarried, they all slumbered and slept. But at midnight there is a cry, Behold, the bridegroom! Come ye forth to meet him. Then all those virgins arose, and trimmed their lamps. And the foolish said unto the wise, Give us of your oil; for our lamps are going out. But the wise answered, saying, Peradventure there will not be enough for us and you: go ye rather to them that sell, and buy for yourselves. And while they went away to buy, the bridegroom came; and they that were ready went in with him to the marriage feast: and the door was shut. Afterward come also the other virgins, saying, Lord, Lord, open to us. But he answered and said, Verily I say unto you, I know you not. Watch therefore, for ye know not the day nor the hour.

Parable of the Foolish Virgins

St. Matthew XI

6. For it is as when a man, going into another country, called his own servants, and delivered unto them his goods. And unto one he gave five talents, to another two, to another one; to each according to his several ability; and he went on his journey. Straightway he that received the five talents went and traded with them, and made other five talents. In like manner he also that received the two gained other two. But he that received the one went away and digged in the earth, and hid his lord's money. Now after a long time the lord of those servants cometh, and maketh a reckoning with them. And he that received the five talents came and brought other five talents, saying, Lord, thou deliveredst unto me five talents: lo, I have gained other five talents. His lord said unto him, Well done, good and faithful servant: thou hast been faithful over a few things, I will set thee over many things: enter thou into the joy of thy lord. And he also that received the two talents came and said, Lord, thou deliveredst unto me two talents: lo, I have gained other two talents. His lord said unto him, Well done, good and faithful servant; thou hast been faithful over a few things, I will set thee over many things: enter thou into the joy of thy lord. And he also that had received the one talent came and said, Lord, I knew thee that thou art a hard man, reaping where thou didst not sow, and gathering where thou didst not scatter: and I was afraid, and went away and hid thy

and Work: Parable of the Talents

talent in the earth: lo, thou hast thine own. But his lord answered and said unto him, Thou wicked and slothful servant, thou knewest that I reap where I sowed not, and gather where I did not scatter; thou oughtest therefore to have put my money to the bankers, and at my coming I should have received back mine own with interest. Take ye away therefore the talent from him, and give it unto him that hath the ten talents. For unto every one that hath shall be given, and he shall have abundance: but from him that hath not, even that which he hath shall be taken away. And cast ye out the unprofitable servant into the outer darkness: there shall be the weeping and gnashing of teeth.

7. But when the Son of man shall come in his glory, and all the angels with him, then shall he sit on the throne of his glory: and before him shall be gathered all the nations: and he shall separate them one from another, as the shepherd separateth the sheep from the goats: and he shall set the sheep on his right hand, but the goats on the left. Then shall the King say unto them on his right hand, Come, ye blessed of my Father, inherit the kingdom prepared for you from the foundation of the world: for I was an hungred, and ye gave me meat: I was thirsty, and ye gave me drink: I was a stranger, and ye took me in; naked, and ye clothed me: I was sick, and ye visited me: I was in prison, and ye came unto me. Then shall the righteous

The Final Judgment

answer him, saying, Lord, when saw we thee an hungred, and fed thee? or athirst, and gave thee drink? And when saw we thee a stranger, and took thee in? or naked, and clothed thee? And when saw we thee sick, or in prison, and came unto thee? And the King shall answer and say unto them, Verily I say unto you, Inasmuch as ye did it unto one of these my brethren, even these least, ye did it unto me. Then shall he say also unto them on the left hand, Depart from me, ye cursed, into the eternal fire which is prepared for the devil and his angels: for I was an hungred, and ye gave me no meat: I was thirsty, and ye gave me no drink: I was a stranger, and ye took me not in; naked, and ye clothed me not; sick, and in prison, and ye visited me not. Then shall they also answer, saying, Lord, when saw we thee an hungred, or athirst, or a stranger, or naked, or sick, or in prison, and did not minister unto thee? Then shall he answer them, saying, Verily I say unto you, Inasmuch as ye did it not unto one of these least, ye did it not unto me. And these shall go away into eternal punishment: but the righteous into eternal life.

XII

THE PASSION AND RESURRECTION OF JESUS

i

And it came to pass, when Jesus had finished all these words, he said unto his disciples, Ye know that after two days the passover cometh, and the Son of man is delivered up to be crucified. Then were gathered together the chief priests, and the elders of the people, unto the court of the high priest, who was called Caiaphas; and they took counsel together that they might take Jesus by subtilty, and kill him. But they said, Not during the feast, lest a tumult arise among the people.

Preparation for the end

Now when Jesus was in Bethany, in the house of Simon the leper, there came unto him a woman having an alabaster cruse of exceeding precious ointment, and she poured it upon his head, as he sat at meat. But when the disciples saw it, they had indignation, saying, To what purpose is this waste? For this ointment might have been sold for much, and given to the poor. But Jesus perceiving it said unto them, Why trouble ye the woman? for she hath wrought a good work upon me. For ye have the poor always with you; but me ye have not always. For in that she poured this ointment upon my body, she did it to prepare me for burial. Verily I say unto you, Wheresoever this gospel shall be preached in the whole world, that also which this woman hath done shall be spoken of for a memorial of her.

Then one of the twelve, who was called Judas Iscariot, went unto the chief priests, and said, What are ye willing to give me, and I will deliver him unto you? And they weighed unto him thirty pieces of silver. And from that time he sought opportunity to deliver him unto them.

ii

Now on the first day of unleavened bread the disciples came to Jesus, saying, Where wilt thou that we make ready for thee to eat the Passover? And he said, Go into the city to such a man, and say unto him, The Master saith, My time is at hand; I keep the Passover at thy house with my disciples. And the disciples did as Jesus appointed them; and they made ready the Passover. Now when even was come, he was sitting at meat with the twelve disciples; and as they were eating, he said, Verily I say unto you, that one of you shall betray me. And they were exceeding sorrowful,

The Last Supper

and began to say unto him every one, Is it I, Lord? And he answered and said, He that dipped his hand with me in the dish, the same shall betray me. The Son of man goeth, even as it is written of him: but woe unto that man through whom the Son of man is betrayed! good were it for that man if he had not been born. And Judas, which betrayed him, answered and said, Is it I, Rabbi? He saith unto him, Thou hast said. And as they were eating, Jesus took bread, and blessed, and brake it; and he gave to the disciples, and said, Take, eat; this is my body. And he took a cup, and gave thanks, and gave to them, saying, Drink ye all of it; for this is my blood of the covenant, which is shed for many unto remission of sins. But I say unto you, I will not drink henceforth of this fruit of the vine, until that day when I drink it new with you in my Father's kingdom.

iii

And when they had sung a hymn, they went out unto the mount of Olives.

Then saith Jesus unto them, All ye shall be offended in me this night: for it is written, *I will smite the shepherd and the sheep of the flock shall be scattered abroad*. But after I am raised up, I will go before you into Galilee. But Peter answered and said unto him, If all shall be offended in thee, I will never be offended. Jesus said unto him, Verily I say unto

The Arrest on Olivet

St. Matthew XII iii

thee, that this night, before the cock crow, thou shalt deny me thrice. Peter saith unto him, Even if I must die with thee, yet will I not deny thee. Likewise also said all the disciples.

Then cometh Jesus with them unto a place called Gethsemane, and saith unto his disciples, Sit ye here, while I go yonder and pray. And he took with him Peter and the two sons of Zebedee, and began to be sorrowful and sore troubled. Then saith he unto them, My soul is exceeding sorrowful, even unto death: abide ye here, and watch with me. And he went forward a little, and fell on his face, and prayed, saying, O my Father, if it be possible, let this cup pass away from me: nevertheless, not as I will, but as thou wilt. And he cometh unto the disciples, and findeth them sleeping, and saith unto Peter, What, could ye not watch with me one hour? Watch and pray, that ye enter not into temptation: the spirit indeed is willing, but the flesh is weak. Again a second time he went away, and prayed, saying, O my Father, if this cannot pass away, except I drink it, thy will be done. And he came again and found them sleeping, for their eyes were heavy. And he left them again, and went away, and prayed a third time, saying again the same words. Then cometh he to the disciples, and saith unto them, Sleep on now, and take your rest: behold, the hour is at hand, and the Son of man is betrayed unto the hands of sinners. Arise, let us be going: behold, he is at hand that betrayeth me.

And while he yet spake, lo, Judas, one of the twelve, came, and with him a great multitude with swords and staves, from the chief priests and elders of the people. Now he that betrayed him gave them a sign, saying, Whomsoever I shall kiss, that is he: take him. And straightway he came to Jesus, and said, Hail, Rabbi; and kissed him. And Jesus said unto him, Friend, do that for which thou art come. Then they came and laid hands on Jesus, and took him. And behold, one of them that were with Jesus stretched out his hand, and drew his sword, and smote the servant of the high priest, and struck off his ear. Then saith Jesus unto him, Put up again thy sword into its place: for all they that take the sword shall perish with the sword. Or thinkest thou that I cannot beseech my Father, and he shall even now send me more than twelve legions of angels? How then should the scriptures be fulfilled, that thus it must be? In that hour said Jesus to the multitudes, Are ye come out as against a robber with swords and staves to seize me? I sat daily in the temple teaching, and ye took me not. But all this is come to pass, that the scriptures of the prophets might be fulfilled. Then all the disciples left him, and fled.

And they that had taken Jesus led him away to the house of Caiaphas the high priest, where the scribes and the elders were gathered together. But Peter followed him afar off, unto the court of the high priest, and entered in, and sat with the officers, to see the end. Now the chief

St. Matthew   XII iii

priests and the whole council sought false witness against
Jesus, that they might put him to death; and they found
it not, though many false witnesses came.
But afterward came two, and said, This man   The Exami-
said, I am able to destroy the temple of God, nation before
and to build it in three days. And the   Caiaphas
high priest stood up, and said unto him, Answerest thou
nothing? what is it which these witness against thee? But
Jesus held his peace. And the high priest said unto him,
I adjure thee by the living God, that thou tell us whether
thou be the Christ, the Son of God. Jesus saith unto him,
Thou hast said: nevertheless I say unto you, Henceforth
ye shall see the Son of man sitting at the right hand of
power, and coming on the clouds of heaven. Then the
high priest rent his garments, saying, He hath spoken
blasphemy: what further need have we of witnesses? behold, now ye have heard the blasphemy: what think ye?
They answered and said, He is worthy of death. Then
did they spit in his face and buffet him: and some smote
him with the palms of their hands, saying, Prophesy unto
us, thou Christ: who is he that struck thee?

Now Peter was sitting without in the court: and a maid
came unto him, saying, Thou also wast with Jesus the
Galilæan. But he denied before them all, saying, I know
not what thou sayest. And when he was gone out into
the porch, another maid saw him, and saith unto them
that were there, This man also was with Jesus the Naza-

rene. And again he denied with an oath, I know not the man. And after a little while they that stood by came and said to Peter, Of a truth thou also art one of them; for thy speech bewrayeth thee. Then began he to curse and to swear, I know not the man. And straightway the cock crew. And Peter remembered the word which Jesus had said, Before the cock crow, thou shalt deny me thrice. And he went out, and wept bitterly.

iv

Now when morning was come, all the chief priests and the elders of the people took counsel against Jesus to put him to death: and they bound him, and led him away, and delivered him up to Pilate the governor.

The Trial before Pilate

Then Judas, which betrayed him, when he saw that he was condemned, repented himself, and brought back the thirty pieces of silver to the chief priests and elders, saying, I have sinned in that I betrayed innocent blood. But they said, What is that to us? see thou to it. And he cast down the pieces of silver into the sanctuary, and departed; and he went away and hanged himself. And the chief priests took the pieces of silver, and said, It is not lawful to put them into the treasury, since it is the price of blood. And they took counsel, and bought with them the potter's field, to bury strangers in. Wherefore that field was called, The field of blood, unto this day. Then was fulfilled that which was spoken by Jeremiah the prophet, saying, *And they took the thirty pieces of silver, the price of him that was priced, whom certain of the children of Israel did price; and they gave them for the potter's field, as the Lord appointed me.*

Now Jesus stood before the governor: and the governor asked him, saying, Art thou the King of the Jews? And Jesus said unto him, Thou sayest. And when he was accused by the chief priests and elders, he answered nothing. Then saith Pilate unto him, Hearest thou not how many things they witness against thee? And he gave him no answer, not even to one word: insomuch that the governor marvelled greatly. Now at the feast the governor was wont to release unto the multitude one prisoner, whom they would. And they had then a notable prisoner, called Barabbas. When therefore they were gathered together, Pilate said unto them, Whom will ye that I release unto you? Barabbas, or Jesus which is called Christ? For he knew that for envy they had delivered him up. And while he was sitting on the judgement-seat, his wife sent unto him, saying, Have thou nothing to do with that righteous man: for I have suffered many things this day in a dream because of him. Now the chief priests and the elders persuaded the multitudes that they should ask for Barabbas, and destroy Jesus. But the governor answered and said unto them, Whether of the twain will ye that I release unto you? And they said, Barabbas. Pilate saith unto them, What then shall I do unto Jesus which is called Christ? They all say, Let him be crucified. And he said, Why, what evil hath he done? But they cried out exceedingly, saying, Let him be crucified. So when Pilate saw that he prevailed nothing, but rather that a tumult was arising, he took water, and washed his hands before the multitude, saying, I am innocent of the blood of this righteous man: see ye to it. And all the people answered and said, His blood be on us, and on our children. Then released he unto them Barabbas: but Jesus he scourged and delivered to be crucified.

V

Then the soldiers of the governor took Jesus into the palace, and gathered unto him the whole band. And they stripped him, and put on him a scarlet robe. And they plaited a crown of thorns and put it upon his head, and a reed in his right hand; and they kneeled down before him, and mocked him, saying, Hail, King of the Jews! And they spat upon him, and took the reed and smote him on the head. And when they had mocked him, they took off from him the robe, and put on him his garments, and led him away to crucify him.

The Crucifixion

And as they came out, they found a man of Cyrene, Simon by name: him they compelled to go with them, that he might bear his cross. And when they were come unto a place called *Golgotha*, that is to say, The place of a skull, they gave him wine to drink mingled with gall: and when he had tasted it, he would not drink. And when they had crucified him, they parted his garments among them, casting lots: and they sat and watched him there. And they set up over his head his accusation written:

> This is Jesus
> The King of the Jews

Then are there crucified with him two robbers, one on the right hand, and one on the left. And they that passed by railed on him, wagging their heads, and saying, Thou that destroyest the temple, and buildest it in three days, save thyself: if thou art the Son of God, come down from the cross. In like manner also the chief priests mocking him, with the scribes and elders, said, He saved others; himself he cannot save. He is the King of Israel; let him now come down from the cross, and we will believe on him. He trusteth on God; let him deliver him now, if he desireth him: for he said, I am the Son of God. And the robbers also that were crucified with him cast upon him the same reproach.

Now from the sixth hour there was darkness over all the land until the ninth hour. And about the ninth hour Jesus cried with a loud voice, saying, *Eli, Eli, lama sabachthani?* that is, My God, my God, why hast thou forsaken me? And some of them that stood there, when they heard it, said, This man calleth Elijah. And straightway one of them ran, and took a sponge, and filled it with vinegar, and put it on a reed, and gave him to drink. And the rest said, Let be; let us see whether Elijah cometh to save him. And Jesus cried again with a loud voice, and yielded up his spirit. And behold, the veil of the temple was rent in twain from the top to the bottom; and the earth did quake; and the rocks were rent; and the tombs were opened; and many bodies of the saints that had fallen asleep were raised; and coming forth out of the tombs after his resurrection they entered into the holy city and appeared unto many. Now the centurion, and they that were with him watching Jesus, when they saw the earthquake, and the things that were done, feared exceedingly, saying, Truly this was the Son of God. And many women were there beholding from afar, which had followed Jesus from Galilee, ministering unto him: among whom was Mary Magdalene, and Mary the mother of James and Joses, and the mother of the sons of Zebedee.

vi

And when even was come, there came a rich man from Arimathæa, named Joseph, who also himself was Jesus' disciple: this man went to Pilate, and asked for the body of Jesus. Then Pilate commanded it to be given up. And

Joseph took the body, and wrapped it in a clean linen cloth, and laid it in his own new tomb, which he had hewn out in the rock: and he rolled a great stone to the door of the tomb, and departed. **The Burial**
And Mary Magdalene was there, and the other Mary, sitting over against the sepulchre.

Now on the morrow, which is the day after the Preparation, the chief priests and the Pharisees were gathered together unto Pilate, saying, Sir, we remember that that deceiver said, while he was yet alive, After three days I rise again. Command therefore that the sepulchre be made sure until the third day, lest haply his disciples come and steal him away, and say unto the people, He is risen from the dead: and the last error will be worse than the first. Pilate said unto them, Ye have a guard: go your way, make it as sure as ye can. So they went, and made the sepulchre sure, sealing the stone, the guard being with them.

vii

Now late on the sabbath day, as it began to dawn toward the first day of the week, came Mary Magdalene and the other Mary to see the sepulchre.
And behold, there was a great earthquake; for an angel of the Lord descended from heaven, and came and rolled away the stone, and sat upon it. His appearance was as lightning, and **The Resurrection and Ascension**

his raiment white as snow: and for fear of him the watchers did quake, and became as dead men. And the angel answered and said unto the women, Fear not ye: for I know that ye seek Jesus, which hath been crucified. He is not here; for he is risen, even as he said. Come, see the place where the Lord lay. And go quickly, and tell his disciples, He is risen from the dead; and lo, he goeth before you into Galilee; there shall ye see him: lo, I have told you. And they departed quickly from the tomb with fear and great joy, and ran to bring his disciples word. And behold, Jesus met them, saying, All hail. And they came and took hold of his feet, and worshipped him. Then saith Jesus unto them, Fear not: go tell my brethren that they depart into Galilee, and there shall they see me.

Now while they were going, behold, some of the guard came into the city, and told unto the chief priests all the things that were come to pass. And when they were assembled with the elders, and had taken counsel, they gave large money unto the soldiers, saying, Say ye, His disciples came by night, and stole him away while we slept. And if this come to the governor's ears, we will persuade him, and rid you of care. So they took the money, and did as they were taught: and this saying was spread abroad among the Jews, and continueth until this day.

But the eleven disciples went into Galilee, unto the

mountain where Jesus had appointed them. And when they saw him, they worshipped him: but some doubted. And Jesus came to them and spake unto them, saying: All authority hath been given unto me in heaven and on earth. Go ye therefore, and make disciples of all the nations, baptizing them into the name of the Father and of the Son and of the Holy Ghost: teaching them to observe all things whatsoever I commanded you: and lo, I am with you alway, even unto the end of the world.

THE GOOD TIDINGS
(GOSPEL)

OR

THE ACTS AND SAYINGS OF JESUS

ACCORDING TO

ST. MARK

i

THE beginning of the gospel of Jesus Christ, the Son of God.

Even as it is written in Isaiah the prophet,

> *Behold, I send my messenger before thy face, who shall prepare thy way;*

> *The voice of one crying in the wilderness,*
> *Make ye ready the way of the Lord,*
> *Make his paths straight;*

John came, who baptized in the wilderness and preached the baptism of repentance unto remission of sins. And there went out unto him all the country of Judæa, and all they of Jerusalem; and they were baptized of him in the river Jordan, confessing their sins. And John was clothed with camel's hair, and had a leathern girdle about his loins, and did eat locusts and wild honey. And he preached, saying, There cometh after me he that is mightier than I, the latchet of whose shoes I am not worthy to stoop down and unloose. I baptized you with water; but he shall baptize you with the Holy Ghost.

And it came to pass in those days, that Jesus came

from Nazareth of Galilee, and was baptized of John in the Jordan. And straightway coming up out of the water, he saw the heavens rent asunder, and the Spirit as a dove descending upon him: and a voice came out of the heavens, Thou art my beloved Son, in thee I am well pleased.

And straightway the Spirit driveth him forth into the wilderness. And he was in the wilderness forty days tempted of Satan; and he was with the wild beasts; and the angels ministered unto him.

ii

Now after that John was delivered up, Jesus came into Galilee, preaching the gospel of God, and saying, **The time is fulfilled, and the kingdom of God is at hand: repent ye, and believe in the gospel.**

And passing along by the sea of Galilee, he saw Simon and Andrew the brother of Simon casting a net in the sea: for they were fishers. And Jesus said unto them, **Come ye after me, and I will make you to become fishers of men.** And straightway they left the nets, and followed him. And going on a little further, he saw James the son of Zebedee, and John his brother, who also were in the boat mending the nets. And straightway he called them: and they left their father Zebedee in the boat with the hired servants, and went after him.

And they go into Capernaum; and straightway on the sabbath day he entered into the synagogue and taught. And they were astonished at his teaching: for he taught them as having authority, and not as the scribes. And straightway there was in their synagogue a man with an unclean spirit; and he cried out, saying, What have we to do with thee, thou Jesus of Nazareth? art thou come to destroy us? I know thee who thou art, the Holy One of God. And Jesus rebuked him, saying, Hold thy peace, and come out of him. And the unclean spirit, tearing him and crying with a loud voice, came out of him. And they were all amazed, insomuch that they questioned among themselves, saying, What is this? a new teaching! with authority he commandeth even the unclean spirits, and they obey him. And the report of him went out straightway everywhere into all the region of Galilee round about.

And straightway, when they were come out of the synagogue, they came into the house of Simon and Andrew, with James and John. Now Simon's wife's mother lay sick of a fever; and straightway they tell him of her: and he came and took her by the hand, and raised her up; and the fever left her, and she ministered unto them.

And at even, when the sun did set, they brought unto him all that were sick, and them that were possessed with devils. And all the city was gathered together at the door. And he healed many that were sick with divers diseases, and cast out many devils; and he suffered not the devils to speak, because they knew him.

And in the morning, a great while before day, he rose up and went out, and departed into a desert place, and there prayed. And Simon and they that were with him followed after him; and they found him, and say unto him, All are seeking thee. And he saith unto them, Let us go elsewhere into the next towns, that I may preach there also; for to this end came I forth. And he went into their synagogues throughout all Galilee, preaching and casting out devils.

iii

And there cometh to him a leper, beseeching him, and kneeling down to him, and saying unto him, If thou wilt, thou canst make me clean. And being moved with compassion, he stretched forth his hand, and touched him, and saith unto him, I will; be thou made clean. And straightway the leprosy departed from him, and he was made clean. And he sternly charged him, and straightway sent him out, and saith unto him, See thou say nothing to any man: but go thy way, shew thyself to the priest, and offer for thy cleansing the things which Moses commanded, for a testimony unto them. But he went out, and began to publish it much, and to spread abroad the matter, insomuch that Jesus could no more openly enter into a

St. Mark iii

city, but was without in desert places: and they came to him from every quarter.

And when he entered again into Capernaum after some days, it was noised that he was in the house. And many were gathered together, so that there was no longer room for them, no, not even about the door: and he spake the word unto them. And they come, bringing unto him a man sick of the palsy, borne of four. And when they could not come nigh unto him for the crowd, they uncovered the roof where he was: and when they had broken it up, they let down the bed whereon the sick of the palsy lay. And Jesus seeing their faith saith unto the sick of the palsy, Son, thy sins are forgiven. But there were certain of the scribes sitting there, and reasoning in their hearts, Why doth this man thus speak? he blasphemeth: who can forgive sins but one, even God? And straightway Jesus, perceiving in his spirit that they so reasoned within themselves, saith unto them, Why reason ye these things in your hearts? Whether is easier, to say to the sick of the palsy, Thy sins are forgiven; or to say, Arise, and take up thy bed, and walk? But that ye may know that the Son of man hath power on earth to forgive sins (he saith to the sick of the palsy), I say unto thee, Arise, take up thy bed, and go unto thy house. And he arose, and straightway took up the bed, and went forth before them all; insomuch that they were all amazed, and glorified God, saying, We never saw it on this fashion.

iv

And he went forth again by the sea side; and all the multitude resorted unto him, and he taught them. And as he passed by, he saw Levi the son of Alphæus sitting at the place of toll, and he saith unto him, Follow me. And he arose and followed him. And it came to pass, that he was sitting at meat in his house, and many publicans and sinners sat down with Jesus and his disciples: for there were many, and they followed him. And the scribes of the Pharisees, when they saw that he was eating with the sinners and publicans, said unto his disciples, He eateth and drinketh with publicans and sinners. And when Jesus heard it, he saith unto them: **They that are whole have no need of a physician, but they that are sick: I came not to call the righteous, but sinners.**

And John's disciples and the Pharisees were fasting: and they come and say unto him, Why do John's disciples and the disciples of the Pharisees fast, but thy disciples fast not? And Jesus said unto them: **Can the sons of the bridechamber fast, while the bridegroom is with them?** as long as they have the bridegroom with them, they cannot fast. But the days will come, when the bridegroom shall be taken away from them, and then will they fast in that day. No man seweth a piece of undressed cloth on an old garment: else that which should fill it up taketh from it, the new from the old, and a worse rent is made. And no man putteth new wine into old wine-skins: else the wine will burst the skins, and the wine perisheth, and the skins: but they put new wine into fresh wine-skins.

V

And it came to pass, that he was going on the sabbath day through the cornfields; and his disciples began, as they went, to pluck the ears of corn. And the Pharisees said unto him, Behold, why do they on the sabbath day that which is not lawful? And he said unto them: **Did ye never read what David did, when he had need, and was an hungred, he, and they that were with him?** How he entered into the house of God when Abiathar was high priest, and did eat the shewbread, which it is not lawful to eat save for the priests, and gave also to them that were with him? And he said unto them, The sabbath was made for man, and not man for the sabbath: so that the Son of man is lord even of the sabbath.

And he entered again into the synagogue; and there was a man there which had his hand withered. And they watched him, whether he would heal him on the sabbath day; that they might accuse him. And he saith unto the man that had his hand withered, Stand forth. And he saith unto them, Is it lawful on the sabbath day to do good, or to do harm? to save a life, or to kill? But they held their peace. And when he had looked round about on them with anger, being grieved at the hardening of their heart, he saith unto the man, Stretch forth thy hand. And he stretched it forth: and his hand was restored. And the Pharisees went out, and straightway with the Herodians took counsel against him, how they might destroy him.

vi

And Jesus with his disciples withdrew to the sea: and a great multitude from Galilee followed: and from Judæa, and from Jerusalem, and from Idumæa, and beyond Jordan, and about Tyre and Sidon, a great multitude, hearing what great things he did, came unto him. And he spake to his disciples, that a little boat should wait on him because of the crowd, lest they should throng him: for he had healed many; insomuch that as many as had plagues pressed upon him that they might touch him. And the unclean spirits, whensoever they beheld him, fell down before him, and cried, saying, Thou art the Son of God. And he charged them much that they should not make him known. And he goeth up into the mountain, and calleth unto him whom he himself would: and they went unto him. And he appointed twelve, that they might be with him, and that he might send them forth to preach, and to have authority to cast out devils: and Simon he surnamed Peter; and James the son of Zebedee, and John the brother of James; and them he surnamed Boanerges, which is, Sons of thunder: and Andrew, and Philip, and Bartholomew, and Matthew, and Thomas, and James the son of Alphæus, and Thaddæus, and Simon the Cananæan; and Judas Iscariot, which also betrayed him.

vii

And he cometh into a house. And the multitude cometh together again, so that they could not so much as eat bread. And when his friends heard it, they went out to lay hold on him: for they said, He is beside himself. And the scribes which came down from Jerusalem said, He hath Beelzebub, and, By the prince of the devils casteth he out the devils. And he called them unto him, and said unto them in parables: **How can Satan cast out Satan?** And if a kingdom be divided against itself, that kingdom cannot stand. And if a house be divided against itself, that house will not be able to stand. And if Satan hath risen up against himself, and is divided, he cannot stand, but hath an end. But no one can enter into the house of the strong man, and spoil his goods, except he first bind the strong man; and then he will spoil his house. Verily I say unto you, All their sins shall be forgiven unto the sons of men, and their blasphemies wherewith soever they shall blaspheme: but whosoever shall blaspheme against the Holy Spirit hath never forgiveness, but is guilty of an eternal sin: because they said, He hath an unclean spirit.

viii ⇥ The Gospel

And there come his mother and his brethren; and, standing without, they sent unto him, calling him. And a multitude was sitting about him; and they say unto him, Behold, thy mother and thy brethren without seek for thee. And he answereth them, and saith, Who is my mother and my brethren? And looking round on them which sat round about him, he saith, **Behold, my mother and my brethren! For whosoever shall do the will of God, the same is my brother, and sister, and mother.**

viii

1. And again he began to teach by the sea side. And there is gathered unto him a very great multitude, so that he entered into a boat, and sat in the sea; and all the multitude were by the sea on the land. And he taught them many things in parables, and said unto them in his teaching, Hearken: Behold, the sower went forth to sow: and it came to pass, as he sowed, some seed fell by the way side, and the birds came and devoured it. And other fell on the rocky ground, where it had not much earth; and straightway it sprang up, because it had no deepness of earth: and when the sun was risen, it was scorched; and because it had no root, it withered away. And other fell among the thorns, and the thorns grew up, and choked it, and it yielded no fruit. And others fell into the good ground, and yielded fruit, growing up and increasing; and

brought forth, thirtyfold, and sixtyfold, and a hundredfold. And he said, Who hath ears to hear, let him hear.

2. And when he was alone, they that were about him with the twelve asked of him the parables. And he said unto them: Unto you is given the mystery of the kingdom of God: but unto them that are without, all things are done in parables: that seeing they may see, and not perceive; and hearing they may hear, and not understand; lest haply they should turn again, and it should be forgiven them. And he saith unto them: Know ye not this parable? and how shall ye know all the parables? The sower soweth the word. And these are they by the way side, where the word is sown; and when they have heard, straightway cometh Satan, and taketh away the word which hath been sown in them. And these in like manner are they that are sown upon the rocky places, who, when they have heard the word, straightway receive it with joy; and they have no root in themselves, but endure for a while; then, when tribulation or persecution ariseth because of the word, straightway they stumble. And others are they that are sown among the thorns; these are they that have heard the word, and the cares of the world, and the deceitfulness of riches, and the lusts of other things entering in, choke the word, and it becometh unfruitful. And those are they that were sown upon the good ground; such as hear the word, and accept it, and bear fruit, thirtyfold, and sixtyfold, and a hundredfold.

And he said unto them: Is the lamp brought to be put under the bushel, or under the bed, and not to be put on the stand? For there is nothing hid, save that it should be manifested; neither was anything made secret, but that it should come to light. If any man hath ears to hear, let him hear. And he said unto them, Take heed what ye hear: with what measure ye mete it shall be measured unto you: and more shall be given unto you. For he that hath, to him shall be given: and he that hath not, from him shall be taken away even that which he hath.

3. And he said: So is the kingdom of God, as if a man should cast seed upon the earth; and should sleep and rise night and day, and the seed should spring up and grow, he knoweth not how. The earth beareth fruit of herself; first the blade, then the ear, then the full corn in the ear. But when the fruit is ripe, straightway he putteth forth the sickle, because the harvest is come.

And he said: How shall we liken the kingdom of God? or in what parable shall we set it forth? It is like a grain of mustard seed, which, when it is sown upon the earth, though it be less than all the seeds that are upon the earth, yet when it is sown, groweth up, and becometh greater than all the herbs, and putteth out great branches; so that the birds of the heaven can lodge under the shadow thereof.

And with many such parables spake he the word unto them, as they were able to hear it: and without a parable spake he not unto them: but privately to his own disciples he expounded all things.

ix

And on that day, when even was come, he saith unto them, Let us go over unto the other side. And leaving the multitude, they take him with them, even as he was, in the boat. And other boats were with him. And there ariseth a great storm of wind, and the waves beat into the boat, insomuch that the boat was now filling. And he himself was in the stern, asleep on the cushion: and they awake him, and say unto him, Master, carest thou not that we perish? And he awoke, and rebuked the wind, and said unto the sea, Peace, be still. And the wind ceased, and there was a great calm. And he said unto them, Why are ye fearful? have ye not yet faith? And they feared exceedingly, and said one to another, Who then is this, that even the wind and the sea obey him?

And they came to the other side of the sea, into the country of the Gerasenes. And when he was come out of the boat, straightway there met him out of the tombs a man with an unclean spirit, who had his dwelling in the tombs: and no man could any more bind him, no, not with a chain; because that he had been often bound with fetters and chains, and the chains had been rent asunder by him, and the fetters broken in pieces: and no man had strength to tame him. And always, night and day, in the tombs and in the mountains, he was crying out, and cutting himself with stones. And when he saw Jesus from afar, he ran and worshipped him; and crying out with a loud voice, he saith, What have I to do with thee, Jesus, thou Son of the Most High God? I adjure thee by God, torment me not. For he said unto him, Come forth, thou unclean spirit, out of the man. And he asked him, What is thy name? And he saith unto him, My name is Legion; for we are many. And he besought him much that he would not send them away out of the country. Now there was there on the mountain side a great herd of swine feeding. And they besought him, saying, Send us into the swine, that we may enter into them. And he gave them leave. And the unclean spirits came out, and entered into the swine: and the herd rushed down the steep into the sea, in number about two thousand; and they were choked in the sea. And they that fed them fled, and told it in the city, and in the country. And they came to see what it was that had come to pass. And they come to Jesus, and behold him that was possessed with devils sitting, clothed and in his right mind, even him that had the legion: and they were afraid. And they that saw it declared unto them how it befell him that was possessed with devils, and concerning the swine. And they began to beseech him to depart from their borders. And as he was entering into the boat, he that had been possessed with devils besought him that he might be with him. And he suffered him

St. Mark

not, but saith unto him, Go to thy house unto thy friends, and tell them how great things the Lord hath done for thee, and how he had mercy on thee. And he went his way, and began to publish in Decapolis how great things Jesus had done for him: and all men did marvel.

And when Jesus had crossed over again in the boat unto the other side, a great multitude was gathered unto him: and he was by the sea. And there cometh one of the rulers of the synagogue, Jaïrus by name; and seeing him, he falleth at his feet, and beseecheth him much, saying, My little daughter is at the point of death: I pray thee, that thou come and lay thy hands on her, that she may be made whole, and live. And he went with him; and a great multitude followed him, and they thronged him.

And a woman, which had an issue of blood twelve years, and had suffered many things of many physicians, and had spent all that she had, and was nothing bettered, but rather grew worse, having heard the things concerning Jesus, came in the crowd behind, and touched his garment. For she said, If I touch but his garments, I shall be made whole. And straightway the fountain of her blood was dried up; and she felt in her body that she was healed of her plague. And straightway Jesus, perceiving in himself that the power proceeding from him had gone forth, turned him about in the crowd, and said, Who touched my garments? And his disciples said unto him, Thou seest the multitude thronging thee, and sayest thou, Who touched me? And he looked round about to see her that had done this thing. But the woman fearing and trembling, knowing what had been done to her, came and fell down before him, and told him all the truth. And he said unto her, Daughter, thy faith hath made thee whole; go in peace, and be whole of thy plague.

While he yet spake, they come from the ruler of the synagogue's house, saying, Thy daughter is dead: why troublest thou the Master any further? But Jesus, not heeding the word spoken, saith unto the ruler of the synagogue, Fear not, only believe. And he suffered no man to follow with him, save Peter, and James, and John the brother of James. And they come to the house of the ruler of the synagogue; and he beholdeth a tumult, and many weeping and wailing greatly. And when he was entered in, he saith unto them, Why make ye a tumult, and weep? the child is not dead, but sleepeth. And they laughed him to scorn. But he, having put them all forth, taketh the father of the child and her mother and them that were with him, and goeth in where the child was. And taking the child by the hand, he saith unto her, *Talitha cumi*; which is, being interpreted, Damsel, I say unto thee, Arise. And straightway the damsel rose up, and walked; for she was twelve years old. And they were amazed straightway with a great amazement. And he charged them much that no man should know this: and he commanded that something should be given her to eat.

x

And he went out from thence; and he cometh into his own country; and his disciples follow him. And when the sabbath was come, he began to teach in the synagogue: and many hearing him were astonished, saying, Whence hath this man these things? and, What is the wisdom that is given unto this man, and what mean such mighty works wrought by his hands? Is not this the carpenter, the son of Mary, and brother of James, and Joses, and Judas, and Simon? and are not his sisters here with us? And they were offended in him. And Jesus said unto them, **A prophet is not without honour, save in his own country, and among his own kin, and in his own house.** And he could there do no mighty work, save that he laid his hands upon a few sick folk, and healed them. And he marvelled because of their unbelief.

xi

And he went round about the villages teaching.

And he called unto him the twelve, and began to send them forth by two and two; and he gave them authority over the unclean spirits; and he charged them that they should take nothing for their journey, save a staff only; no bread, no wallet, no money in their purse; but to go shod with sandals: and, said he, put not on two coats. And he said unto them, Wheresoever ye enter into a house, there abide till ye depart thence. And whatsoever place shall not receive you, and they hear you not, as ye go forth thence, shake off the dust that is under your feet for a testimony unto them. And they went out, and preached that men should repent. And they cast out many devils, and anointed with oil many that were sick, and healed them.

And king Herod heard thereof; for his name had become known: and he said, John the Baptist is risen from the dead, and therefore do these powers work in him. But others said, It is Elijah. And others said, It is a prophet, even as one of the prophets. But Herod, when he heard thereof, said, John, whom I beheaded, he is risen. For Herod himself had sent forth and laid hold upon John, and bound him in prison for the sake of Herodias, his brother Philip's wife: for he had married her. For John said unto Herod, It is not lawful for thee to have thy brother's wife. And Herodias set herself against him, and desired to kill him; and she could not; for Herod feared John, knowing that he was a righteous man and a holy, and kept him safe. And when he heard him, he was much perplexed; and he heard him gladly. And when a convenient day was come, that Herod on his birthday made a supper to his lords, and the high captains, and the chief men of Galilee; and when the daughter of Herodias herself came in and danced, she pleased Herod and them that sat at meat with him; and the king said unto the damsel, Ask of me whatsoever thou wilt, and I will give it thee. And he sware unto her, Whatsoever thou shalt ask of me, I will give it thee, unto the half of my kingdom. And she went out, and said unto her mother, What shall I ask? And she said, The head of John the Baptist. And she came in straightway with haste unto the king, and asked, saying, I will that thou forthwith give me in a charger the head of John the Baptist. And the king was exceeding sorry; but for the sake of his oaths, and of them that sat at meat, he would not reject her. And straightway the king sent forth a soldier of his guard, and commanded to bring his head: and he went and beheaded him in the prison, and brought his head in a charger, and gave it to the damsel; and the damsel gave it to her mother. And when his disciples heard thereof, they came and took up his corpse, and laid it in a tomb.

And the apostles gather themselves together unto Jesus; and they told him all things, whatsoever they had done, and whatsoever they had taught. And he saith unto them, Come ye yourselves apart into a desert place, and rest a while. For there were many coming and going, and they had no leisure so much as to eat. And they went away in the boat to a desert place apart. And the people saw them going, and many knew them, and they ran there together on foot from all the cities, and outwent them.

And he came forth and saw a great multitude, and he had compassion on them, because they were as sheep not having a shepherd: and he began to teach them many things. And when the day was now far spent, his disciples came unto him, and said, The place is desert, and the day is now far spent: send them away, that they may go into the country and villages round about, and buy themselves somewhat to eat. But he answered and said unto them, Give ye them to eat. And they say unto him, Shall we go and buy two hundred pennyworth of bread, and give them to eat? And he saith unto them, How many loaves have ye? go and see. And when they knew, they say, Five, and two fishes. And he commanded them that all should sit down by companies upon the green grass. And they sat down in ranks, by hundreds, and by fifties. And he took the five loaves and the two fishes, and looking up to heaven, he blessed, and brake the loaves; and he gave to the disciples to set before them; and the two fishes divided he among them all. And they did all eat, and were filled. And they took up broken pieces, twelve basketfuls, and also of the fishes. And they that ate the loaves were five thousand men.

And straightway he constrained his disciples to enter into the boat, and to go before him unto the other side to Bethsaida, while he himself sendeth the multitude away. And after he had taken leave of them, he departed into the mountain to pray. And when even was come, the boat was in the midst of the sea, and he alone on the land. And seeing them distressed in rowing, for the wind was contrary unto them, about the fourth watch of the night he cometh unto them, walking on the sea; and he would have passed by them: but they, when they saw him walking on the sea, supposed that it was an apparition, and cried out: for they all saw him, and were troubled. But he straightway spake with them, and saith unto them, Be of good cheer: it is I; be not afraid. And he went up unto them into the boat; and the wind ceased. And they were sore amazed in themselves; for they understood not concerning the loaves, but their heart was hardened.

And when they had crossed over, they came to the land unto Gennesaret, and moored to the shore. And when they were come out of the boat, straightway the people knew him, and ran round about that whole region, and began to carry about on their beds those that were sick, where they heard he was. And wheresoever he entered, into villages, or into cities, or into the country, they laid the sick in the marketplaces, and besought him that they might touch if it were but the border of his garment: and as many as touched him were made whole.

xii

And there are gathered together unto him the Pharisees, and certain of the scribes, which had come from Jerusalem, and had seen that some of his disciples ate their bread with defiled * hands. And the Pharisees and the scribes ask him, Why walk not thy disciples according to the Tradition of the Elders, but eat their bread with defiled hands? And he said unto them: Well did Isaiah prophesy of you hypocrites, as it is written: *This people honoureth me with their lips, but their heart is far from me. But in vain do they worship me, teaching as their doctrines the precepts of men.* Ye leave the commandment of God, and hold fast the tradition of men. And he said unto them, Full well do ye reject the commandment of God, that ye may keep your tradition. For Moses said, Honour thy father and thy mother; and, He that speaketh evil of father or mother, let him die the death: but ye say, If a man shall say to his father or his mother, That wherewith thou mightest have been profited by me is Corban, (that is to say, Given to God,) ye no longer suffer him to do aught for his father or his mother; making void the word of God by your tradition, which ye have delivered: and many such like things ye do. And he called to him the multitude again, and said unto them, Hear me all of you, and understand: there is nothing from without the man, that going into him can defile him: but the things which proceed out of the man are those that defile the man. And when he was

* That is, unwashen. For the Pharisees, and all the Jews, except they wash their hands diligently, eat not, holding the Tradition of the Elders. And when they come from the marketplace, except they wash themselves, they eat not. And many other things there be, which they have received to hold, washings of cups, and pots, and brasen vessels.

entered into the house from the multitude, his disciples asked of him the parable. And he saith unto them: Are ye so without understanding also? Perceive ye not, that whatsoever from without goeth into the man, it cannot defile him; because it goeth not into his heart, but into his belly, and goeth out into the draught? This he said, making all meats clean. And he said: That which proceedeth out of the man, that defileth the man. For from within, out of the heart of men, evil thoughts proceed, fornications, thefts, murders, adulteries, covetings, wickednesses, deceit, lasciviousness, an evil eye, railing, pride, foolishness: all these evil things proceed from within, and defile the man.

xiii

And from thence he arose, and went away into the borders of Tyre and Sidon. And he entered into a house, and would have no man know it: and he could not be hid. But straightway a woman, whose little daughter had an unclean spirit, having heard of him, came and fell down at his feet. Now the woman was a Greek, a Syrophœnician by race. And she besought him that he would cast forth the devil out of her daughter. And he said unto her, Let the children first be filled: for it is not meet to take the children's bread and cast it to the dogs. But she answered and saith unto him, Yea, Lord: even the dogs under the table eat of the children's crumbs. And he said unto her, For this saying go thy way; the devil is gone out of thy daughter. And she went away unto her house, and found the child laid upon the bed, and the devil gone out.

xiv

And again he went out from the borders of Tyre, and came through Sidon unto the sea of Galilee, through the midst of the borders of Decapolis. And they bring unto him one that was deaf, and had an impediment in his speech; and they beseech him to lay his hand upon him. And he took him aside from the multitude privately, and put his fingers into his ears, and he spat, and touched his tongue; and looking up to heaven, he sighed, and saith unto him, *Ephphatha*, that is, Be opened. And his ears were opened, and the bond of his tongue was loosed, and he spake plain. And he charged them that they should tell no man: but the more he charged them, so much the more a great deal they published it. And they were beyond measure astonished, saying, He hath done all things well: he maketh even the deaf to hear, and the dumb to speak.

xv

In those days, when there was again a great multitude, and they had nothing to eat, he called unto him his disciples, and saith unto them, I have compassion on the multitude, because they continue with me now three days, and have nothing to eat: and if I send them away fasting to their home, they will faint in the way; and some of them are come from far. And his disciples answered him, Whence shall one be able to fill these men with bread here in a desert place? And he asked them, How many loaves have ye? And they said, Seven. And he commandeth the multitude to sit down on the ground: and he took the seven loaves, and having given thanks, he brake, and gave to his disciples, to set before them; and they set them before the multitude. And they had a few small fishes: and having blessed them, he commanded to set these also before them. And they did eat, and were filled: and they took up, of broken pieces that remained over, seven baskets. And they were about four thousand: and he sent them away. And straightway he entered into the boat with his disciples, and came into the parts of Dalmanutha.

And the Pharisees came forth, and began to question with him, seeking of him a sign from heaven, tempting him. And he sighed deeply in his spirit, and saith, Why doth this generation seek a sign? verily I say unto you, There shall no sign be given unto this generation. And he left them, and again entering into the boat departed to the other side.

And they forgot to take bread; and they had not in the boat with them more than one loaf. And he charged them, saying, **Take heed, beware of the leaven of the Pharisees** and the leaven of Herod. And they reasoned one with another, saying, We have no bread. And Jesus perceiving it saith unto them, Why reason ye, because ye have no bread? do ye not yet perceive, neither understand? have ye your heart hardened? Having eyes, see ye not? and having ears, hear ye not? and do ye not remember? When I brake the five loaves among the five thousand, how many baskets full of broken pieces took ye up? They say unto him, Twelve. And when the seven among the four thousand, how many basketfuls of broken pieces took ye up? And they say unto him, Seven. And he said unto them, Do ye not yet understand?

xvi

And they come unto Bethsaida. And they bring to him a blind man, and beseech him to touch him. And he took hold of the blind man by the hand, and brought him out of the village; and when he had spit on his eyes, and laid his hands upon him, he asked him, Seest thou aught? And he looked up, and said, I see men; for I behold them as trees, walking. Then again he laid his hands upon his eyes; and he looked stedfastly, and was restored, and saw all things clearly. And he sent him away to his home, saying, Do not even enter into the village.

xvii

And Jesus went forth, and his disciples, into the villages of Cæsarea Philippi: and in the way he asked his disciples, saying unto them, Who do men say that I am? And they told him, saying, John the Baptist: and others, Elijah; but others, One of the prophets. And he asked them, But who say ye that I am? Peter answereth and saith unto him, Thou art the Christ. And he charged them that they should tell no man of him. And he began to teach them, that the Son of man must suffer many things, and be rejected by the elders, and the chief priests, and the scribes, and be killed, and after three days rise again. And he spake the saying openly. And Peter took him, and began to rebuke him. But he turning about, and seeing his disciples, rebuked Peter, and saith, Get thee behind me, Satan: for thou mindest not the things of God, but the things of men. And he called unto him the multitude with his disciples, and said unto them: If any man would come after me, let him deny himself, and take up his cross, and follow me. For whosoever would save his life shall lose it; and whosoever shall lose his life for my sake and the gospel's shall save it. For what doth it profit a man, to gain the whole world, and forfeit his life? For what should a man give in exchange for his life? For whosoever shall be ashamed of me and of my words in this adulterous and sinful generation, the Son of man also shall be ashamed of him, when he cometh in the glory of his Father with the holy angels. And he said unto them, Verily I say unto you, There be some here of them that stand by, which shall in no wise taste of death, till they see the kingdom of God come with power.

And after six days Jesus taketh with him Peter, and James, and John, and bringeth them up into a high mountain apart by themselves: and he was transfigured before them: and his garments became glistering, exceeding white; so as no fuller on earth can whiten them. And there appeared unto them Elijah with Moses: and they were talking with Jesus. And Peter answereth and saith to Jesus, Rabbi, it is good for us to be here: and let us make three tabernacles; one for thee, and one for Moses, and one for Elijah. For he wist not what to answer; for they became sore afraid. And there came a cloud overshadowing them: and there came a voice out of the cloud, This is my beloved Son: hear ye him. And suddenly looking round about, they saw no one any more, save Jesus only with themselves. And as they were coming down from the mountain, he charged them that they should tell no man what things they had seen, save when the Son of man should have risen again from the dead. And they kept the saying, questioning among themselves what the rising again from the dead should mean. And they asked him, saying, The scribes say that Elijah must first come. And he said unto them: **Elijah indeed cometh**

St. Mark

first, and restoreth all things: and how is it written of the Son of man, that he should suffer many things and be set at nought? But I say unto you, that Elijah is come, and they have also done unto him whatsoever they listed, even as it is written of him.

And when they came to the disciples, they saw a great multitude about them, and scribes questioning with them. And straightway all the multitude, when they saw him, were greatly amazed, and running to him saluted him. And he asked them, What question ye with them? And one of the multitude answered him, Master, I brought unto thee my son, which hath a dumb spirit; and wheresoever it taketh him, it dasheth him down: and he foameth, and grindeth his teeth, and pineth away: and I spake to thy disciples that they should cast it out; and they were not able. And he answereth them and saith, O faithless generation, how long shall I be with you? how long shall I bear with you? bring him unto me. And they brought him unto him: and when he saw him, straightway the spirit tare him grievously; and he fell on the ground, and wallowed foaming. And he asked his father, How long time is it since this hath come unto him? And he said, From a child. And oft-times it hath cast him both into the fire and into the waters, to destroy him: but if thou canst do anything, have compassion on us, and help us. And Jesus said unto him, If thou canst! All things are possible to him that believeth. Straightway the father of the child cried out, and said, I believe; help thou mine unbelief. And when Jesus saw that a multitude came running together, he rebuked the unclean spirit, saying unto him, Thou dumb and deaf spirit, I command thee, come out of him, and enter no more into him. And having cried out, and torn him much, he came out: and the child became as one dead; insomuch that the more part said, He is dead. But Jesus took him by the hand, and raised him up; and he arose. And when he was come into the house, his disciples asked him privately, saying, We could not cast it out. And he said unto them, This kind can come out by nothing, save by prayer.

xviii

And they went forth from thence, and passed through Galilee; and he would not that any man should know it. For he taught his disciples, and said unto them, **The Son of man is delivered up into the hands of men, and they shall kill him; and when he is killed, after three days he shall rise again.** But they understood not the saying, and were afraid to ask him.

And they came to Capernaum: and when he was in the house he asked them, What were ye reasoning in the way? But they held their peace: for they had disputed one with another in the way, who was the greatest. And he sat down, and called the twelve; and he saith unto them,

St. Mark — xviii

If any man would be first, he shall be last of all, and minister of all. And he took a little child, and set him in the midst of them: and taking him in his arms, he said unto them, Whosoever shall receive one of such little children in my name, receiveth me: and whosoever receiveth me, receiveth not me, but him that sent me.

John said unto him, Master, we saw one casting out devils in thy name: and we forbade him, because he followed not us. But Jesus said, Forbid him not. For there is no man which shall do a mighty work in my name, and be able quickly to speak evil of me. For he that is not against us is for us. For whosoever shall give you a cup of water to drink, because ye are Christ's, verily I say unto you, he shall in no wise lose his reward. And whosoever shall cause one of these little ones that believe on me to stumble, it were better for him if a great millstone were hanged about his neck, and he were cast into the sea. And if thy hand cause thee to stumble, cut it off: it is good for thee to enter into life maimed, rather than having thy two hands to go into hell, into the unquenchable fire. And if thy foot cause thee to stumble, cut it off: it is good for thee to enter into life halt, rather than having thy two feet to be cast into hell. And if thine eye cause thee to stumble, cast it out: it is good for thee to enter into the kingdom of God with one eye, rather than having two eyes to be cast into hell; where their worm dieth not, and the fire is not quenched. For every one shall be salted with fire. Salt is good: but if the salt have lost its saltness, wherewith will ye season it? Have salt in yourselves, and be at peace one with another.

xix

And he arose from thence, and cometh into the borders of Judæa and beyond Jordan: and multitudes come together unto him again; and, as he was wont, he taught them again. And there came unto him Pharisees, and asked him, Is it lawful for a man to put away his wife? tempting him. And he answered and said unto them, What did Moses command you? And they said, Moses suffered to write a bill of divorcement, and to put her away. But Jesus said unto them, For your hardness of heart he wrote you this commandment. But from the beginning of the creation, 'Male and female made he them.' For this cause shall a man leave his father and mother, and shall cleave to his wife; and the twain shall become one flesh: so that they are no more twain, but one flesh. What therefore God hath joined together, let not man put asunder. And in the house the disciples asked him again of this matter. And he saith unto them, Whosoever shall put away his wife, and marry another, committeth adultery against her: and if she herself shall put away her husband, and marry another, she committeth adultery.

XX

And they brought unto him little children, that he should touch them: and the disciples rebuked them. But when Jesus saw it, he was moved with indignation, and said unto them, Suffer the little children to come unto me; forbid them not: for of such is the kingdom of God. Verily I say unto you, Whosoever shall not receive the kingdom of God as a little child, he shall in no wise enter therein. And he took them in his arms, and blessed them, laying his hands upon them.

xxi

And as he was going forth into the way, there ran one to him, and kneeled to him, and asked him, Good Master, what shall I do that I may inherit eternal life? And Jesus said unto him, Why callest thou me good? none is good save one, even God. Thou knowest the commandments, Do not kill, Do not commit adultery, Do not steal, Do not bear false witness, Do not defraud, Honour thy father and mother. And he said unto him, Master, all these things have I observed from my youth. And Jesus looking upon him loved him, and said unto him, One thing thou lackest: go, sell whatsoever thou hast, and give to the poor, and thou shalt have treasure in heaven: and come, follow me. But his countenance fell at the saying, and he went away sorrowful: for he was one that had great possessions. And Jesus looked round about, and saith unto his disciples, **How hardly shall they that have riches enter into the kingdom of God!** And the disciples were amazed at his words. But Jesus answereth again, and saith unto them, **Children, how hard is it for them that trust in riches to enter into the kingdom of God! It is easier for a camel to go through a needle's eye, than for a rich man to enter into the kingdom of God.** And they were astonished exceedingly, saying unto him, Then who can be saved? Jesus looking upon them saith, **With men it is impossible, but not with God: for all things are possible with God.** Peter began to say unto him, Lo, we have left all, and have followed thee. Jesus said, **Verily I say unto you, There is no man that hath left house, or brethren, or sisters, or mother, or father, or children, or lands, for my sake, and for the gospel's sake, but he shall receive a hundredfold now in this time, houses, and brethren, and sisters, and mothers, and children, and lands, with persecutions; and in the world to come eternal life. But many that are first shall be last; and the last first.**

xxii

And they were in the way, going up to Jerusalem; and Jesus was going before them: and they were amazed; and they that followed were afraid. And he took again the twelve, and began to tell them the things that were to happen unto him, saying, Behold, we go up to Jerusalem; and the Son of man shall be delivered unto the chief priests and the scribes; and they shall condemn him to death, and shall deliver him unto the Gentiles: and they shall mock him, and shall spit upon him, and shall scourge him, and shall kill him; and after three days he shall rise again.

And there come near unto him James and John, the sons of Zebedee, saying unto him, Master, we would that thou shouldest do for us whatsoever we shall ask of thee. And he said unto them, What would ye that I should do for you? And they said unto him, Grant unto us that we may sit, one on thy right hand, and one on thy left hand, in thy glory. But Jesus said unto them, Ye know not what ye ask. Are ye able to drink the cup that I drink? or to be baptized with the baptism that I am baptized with? And they said unto him, We are able. And Jesus said unto them, The cup that I drink ye shall drink; and with the baptism that I am baptized withal shall ye be baptized: but to sit on my right hand or on my left hand is not mine to give: but it is for them for whom it hath been prepared. And when the ten heard it, they began to be moved with indignation concerning James and John. And Jesus called them to him, and saith unto them: Ye know that they which are accounted to rule over the Gentiles lord it over them; and their great ones exercise authority over them. But it is not so among you: but whosoever would become great among you, shall be your minister: and whosoever would be first among you, shall be servant of all. For verily the Son of man came not to be ministered unto, but to minister, and to give his life a ransom for many.

xxiii

And they come to Jericho: and as he went out from Jericho, with his disciples and a great multitude, the son of Timæus, Bartimæus, a blind beggar, was sitting by the way side. And when he heard that it was Jesus of Nazareth, he began to cry out, and say, Jesus, thou son of David, have mercy on me. And many rebuked him, that he should hold his peace: but he cried out the more a great deal, Thou son of David, have mercy on me. And Jesus stood still, and said, Call ye him. And they call the blind man, saying unto him, Be of good cheer: rise, he calleth thee. And he, casting away his garment, sprang up, and came to Jesus. And Jesus answered him, and said, What wilt thou that I should do unto thee? And the blind man said unto him, Rabboni, that I may receive my sight. And Jesus said unto him, Go thy way; thy faith hath made thee whole. And straightway he received his sight, and followed him in the way.

xxiv

And when they draw nigh unto Jerusalem, unto Bethphage and Bethany, at the mount of Olives, he sendeth two of his disciples, and saith unto them, Go your way into the village that is over against you: and straightway as ye enter into it, ye shall find a colt tied, whereon no man ever yet sat; loose him, and bring him. And if any one say unto you, Why do ye this? say ye, The Lord hath need of him; and straightway he will send him back hither. And they went away, and found a colt tied at the door without in the open street; and they loose him. And certain of them that stood there said unto them, What do ye, loosing the colt? And they said unto them even as Jesus had said: and they let them go. And they bring the colt unto Jesus, and cast on him their garments; and he sat upon him. And many spread their garments upon the way; and others branches, which they had cut from the fields. And they that went before, and they that followed, cried, 'Hosanna'—'Blessed is he that cometh in the name of the Lord'—'Blessed is the kingdom that cometh, the kingdom of our father David'—'Hosanna in the highest.'

xxv

And he entered into Jerusalem, into the temple; and when he had looked round about upon all things, it being now eventide, he went out unto Bethany with the twelve.

XXV

And on the morrow, when they were come out from Bethany, he hungered. And seeing a fig tree afar off having leaves, he came, if haply he might find anything thereon: and when he came to it, he found nothing but leaves; for it was not the season of figs. And he answered and said unto it, No man eat fruit from thee henceforward for ever. And his disciples heard it.

And they come to Jerusalem: and he entered into the temple, and began to cast out them that sold and them that bought in the temple, and overthrew the tables of the money-changers, and the seats of them that sold the doves; and he would not suffer that any man should carry a vessel through the temple. And he taught, and said unto them, **Is it not written, My house shall be called a house of prayer for all the nations? but ye have made it a den of robbers.** And the chief priests and the scribes heard it, and sought how they might destroy him: for they feared him, for all the multitude was astonished at his teaching.

And every evening he went forth out of the city.

And as they passed by in the morning, they saw the fig tree withered away from the roots. And Peter calling to remembrance saith unto him, Rabbi, behold, the fig tree which thou cursedst is withered away. And Jesus answering saith unto them: **Have faith in God. Verily I say unto you, Whosoever shall say unto this mountain, Be thou taken up and cast into the sea; and shall not doubt in his heart, but shall believe that what he saith cometh**

St. Mark

to pass; he shall have it. Therefore I say unto you, All things whatsoever ye pray and ask for, believe that ye have received them, and ye shall have them. And whensoever ye stand praying, forgive, if ye have aught against any one; that your Father also which is in heaven may forgive you your trespasses.

xxvi

And they come again to Jerusalem: and as he was walking in the temple, there come to him the chief priests, and the scribes, and the elders; and they said unto him, By what authority doest thou these things? or who gave thee this authority to do these things? And Jesus said unto them, I will ask of you one question, and answer me, and I will tell you by what authority I do these things. The baptism of John, was it from heaven, or from men? answer me. And they reasoned with themselves, saying, If we shall say, From heaven; he will say, Why then did ye not believe him? But should we say, From men— they feared the people: for all verily held John to be a prophet. And they answered Jesus and say, We know not. And Jesus saith unto them, Neither tell I you by what authority I do these things. And he began to speak unto them in parables. A man planted a vineyard, and set a hedge about it, and digged a pit for the winepress, and built a tower, and let it out to husbandmen, and went into another country. And at the season he sent to the husbandmen a servant, that he might receive from the husbandmen of the fruits of the vineyard. And they took him, and beat him, and sent him away empty. And again he sent unto them another servant; and him they wounded in the head, and handled shamefully. And he sent another; and him they killed : and many others; beating some, and killing some. He had yet one, a beloved son : he sent him last unto them, saying, They will reverence my son. But those husbandmen said among themselves, This is the heir; come, let us kill him, and the inheritance shall be ours. And they took him, and killed him, and cast him forth out of the vineyard. What therefore will the lord of the vineyard do ? he will come and destroy the husbandmen, and will give the vineyard unto others. Have ye not read even this scripture :

> *The stone which the builders rejected,*
> *The same was made the head of the corner :*
> *This was from the Lord,*
> *And it is marvellous in our eyes ?*

And they sought to lay hold on him; and they feared the multitude; for they perceived that he spake the parable against them : and they left him, and went away.

xxvii

And they send unto him certain of the Pharisees and of the Herodians, that they might catch him in talk. And when they were come, they say unto him, Master, we know that thou art true, and carest not for any one: for thou regardest not the person of men, but of a truth teachest the way of God: Is it lawful to give tribute unto Cæsar, or not? Shall we give, or shall we not give? But he, knowing their hypocrisy, said unto them, Why tempt ye me? bring me a penny, that I may see it. And they brought it. And he saith unto them, Whose is this image and superscription? And they said unto him, Cæsar's. And Jesus said unto them, **Render unto Cæsar the things that are Cæsar's, and unto God the things that are God's.** And they marvelled greatly at him.

And there come unto him Sadducees, which say that there is no resurrection; and they asked him, saying, Master, Moses wrote unto us, If a man's brother die, and leave a wife behind him, and leave no child, that his brother should take his wife, and raise up seed unto his brother. There were seven brethren: and the first took a wife, and dying left no seed; and the second took her, and died, leaving no seed behind him; and the third likewise: and the seven left no seed. Last of all the woman also died. In the resurrection whose wife shall she be of them? for the seven had her to wife. Jesus said unto them: **Is it** not for this cause that ye err, that ye know not the scriptures, nor the power of God? For when they shall rise from the dead, they neither marry, nor are given in marriage; but are as angels in heaven. But as touching the dead, that they are raised; have ye not read in the book of Moses, in the place concerning the Bush, how God spake unto him, saying, I am the God of Abraham, and the God of Isaac, and the God of Jacob? He is not the God of the dead, but of the living: ye do greatly err.

And one of the scribes came, and heard them questioning together, and knowing that he had answered them well, asked him, What commandment is the first of all? Jesus answered, The first is, Hear, O Israel; The Lord our God, the Lord is one: and thou shalt love the Lord thy God with all thy heart, and with all thy soul, and with all thy mind, and with all thy strength. The second is this, Thou shalt love thy neighbour as thyself. There is none other commandment greater than these. And the scribe said unto him, Of a truth, Master, thou hast well said that He is one; and there is none other but He: and to love Him with all the heart, and with all the understanding, and with all the strength, and to love his neighbour as himself, is much more than all whole burnt offerings and sacrifices. And when Jesus saw that he answered discreetly, he said unto him, Thou art not far from the kingdom of God. And no man after that durst ask him any question.

And Jesus answered and said, as he taught in the

temple: How say the scribes that the Christ is the son of David? David himself said in the Holy Spirit,

The Lord said unto my Lord,
Sit thou on my right hand,
Till I make thine enemies the footstool of thy feet.

David himself calleth him Lord; and whence is he his son? And the common people heard him gladly.

And in his teaching he said: Beware of the scribes, which desire to walk in long robes, and to have salutations in the marketplaces, and chief seats in the synagogues, and chief places at feasts: they which devour widows' houses, and for a pretence make long prayers; these shall receive greater condemnation.

xxviii

And he sat down over against the treasury, and beheld how the multitude cast money into the treasury: and many that were rich cast in much. And there came a poor widow, and she cast in two mites, which make a farthing. And he called unto him his disciples, and said unto them, Verily I say unto you, This poor widow cast in more than all they which are casting into the treasury: for they all did cast in of their superfluity; but she of her want did cast in all that she had, even all her living.

xxix

And as he went forth out of the temple, one of his disciples saith unto him, Master, behold, what manner of stones and what manner of buildings! And Jesus said unto him, Seest thou these great buildings? there shall not be left here one stone upon another, which shall not be thrown down.

And as he sat on the mount of Olives over against the temple, Peter and James and John and Andrew asked him privately, Tell us, when shall these things be? and what shall be the sign when these things are all about to be accomplished? And Jesus began to say unto them:

1. Take heed that no man lead you astray. Many shall come in my name, saying, I am he; and shall lead many astray. And when ye shall hear of wars and rumours of wars, be not troubled: these things must needs come to pass; but the end is not yet. For nation shall rise against nation, and kingdom against kingdom: there shall be earthquakes in divers places; there shall be famines: these things are the beginning of travail. But take ye heed to yourselves: for they shall deliver you up to councils; and in synagogues shall ye be beaten; and before governors and kings shall ye stand for my sake, for a testimony unto them. And the gospel must first be preached unto all the nations. And when they lead you to judgement, and deliver you up, be not anxious beforehand what ye shall speak: but what-

soever shall be given you in that hour, that speak ye: for it is not ye that speak, but the Holy Ghost. And brother shall deliver up brother to death, and the father his child; and children shall rise up against parents, and cause them to be put to death. And ye shall be hated of all men for my name's sake: but he that endureth to the end the same shall be saved.

2. But when ye see the abomination of desolation standing where he ought not (let him that readeth understand), then let them that are in Judæa flee unto the mountains: and let him that is on the housetop not go down, nor enter in, to take anything out of his house: and let him that is in the field not return back to take his cloke. But woe unto them that are with child and to them that give suck in those days! And pray ye that it be not in the winter. For those days shall be tribulation, such as there hath not been the like from the beginning of the creation which God created until now, and never shall be. And except the Lord had shortened the days, no flesh would have been saved: but for the elect's sake, whom he chose, he shortened the days. And then if any man shall say unto you, Lo, here is the Christ; or, Lo, there; believe it not: for there shall arise false Christs and false prophets, and shall shew signs and wonders, that they may lead astray, if possible, the elect. But take ye heed: behold, I have told you all things beforehand.

3. But in those days, after that tribulation, the sun shall

be darkened, and the moon shall not give her light, and the stars shall be falling from heaven, and the powers that are in the heavens shall be shaken. And then shall they see the Son of man coming in clouds with great power and glory. And then shall he send forth the angels, and shall gather together his elect from the four winds, from the uttermost part of the earth to the uttermost part of heaven.

4. Now from the fig tree learn her parable: when her branch is now become tender, and putteth forth its leaves, ye know that the summer is nigh; even so ye also, when ye see these things coming to pass, know ye that he is nigh, even at the doors. Verily I say unto you, This generation shall not pass away, until all these things be accomplished. Heaven and earth shall pass away: but my words shall not pass away. But of that day or that hour knoweth no one, not even the angels in heaven, neither the Son, but the Father.

5. Take ye heed, watch and pray: for ye know not when the time is. It is as when a man, sojourning in another country, having left his house, and given authority to his servants, to each one his work, commanded also the porter to watch. Watch therefore: for ye know not when the lord of the house cometh, whether at even, or at midnight, or at cockcrowing, or in the morning; lest coming suddenly he find you sleeping. And what I say unto you I say unto all, Watch.

XXX

Now after two days was the feast of the Passover and the unleavened bread: and the chief priests and the scribes sought how they might take him with subtilty, and kill him: for they said, Not during the feast, lest haply there shall be a tumult of the people.

And while he was in Bethany in the house of Simon the leper, as he sat at meat, there came a woman having an alabaster cruse of ointment of spikenard very costly; and she brake the cruse, and poured it over his head. But there were some that had indignation among themselves, saying, To what purpose hath this waste of the ointment been made? For this ointment might have been sold for above three hundred pence, and given to the poor. And they murmured against her. But Jesus said, Let her alone; why trouble ye her? she hath wrought a good work on me. For ye have the poor always with you, and whensoever ye will ye can do them good: but me ye have not always. She hath done what she could: she hath anointed my body aforehand for the burying. And verily I say unto you, Wheresoever the gospel shall be preached throughout the whole world, that also which this woman hath done shall be spoken of for a memorial of her.

And Judas Iscariot, he that was one of the twelve, went away unto the chief priests, that he might deliver him unto them. And they, when they heard it, were glad, and promised to give him money. And he sought how he might conveniently deliver him unto them.

xxxi

And on the first day of unleavened bread, when they sacrificed the Passover, his disciples say unto him, Where wilt thou that we go and make ready that thou mayest eat the Passover? And he sendeth two of his disciples, and saith unto them, Go into the city, and there shall meet you a man bearing a pitcher of water: follow him; and wheresoever he shall enter in, say to the goodman of the house, The Master saith, Where is my guest-chamber, where I shall eat the Passover with my disciples? And he will himself shew you a large upper room furnished and ready: and there make ready for us. And the disciples went forth, and came into the city, and found as he had said unto them: and they made ready the Passover.

And when it was evening he cometh with the twelve. And as they sat and were eating, Jesus said, Verily I say unto you, One of you shall betray me, even he that eateth with me. They began to be sorrowful, and to say unto him one by one, Is it I? And he said unto them, It is one of the twelve, he that dippeth with me in the dish. For the Son of man goeth, even as it is written of him: but woe unto that man through whom the Son of man is betrayed! good were it for that man if he had not been born.

And as they were eating, he took bread, and when he had blessed, he brake it, and gave to them, and said, Take ye: this is my body. And he took a cup, and when he had given thanks, he gave to them: and they all drank of it. And he said unto them, This is my blood of the covenant, which is shed for many. Verily I say unto you, I will no more drink of the fruit of the vine, until that day when I drink it new in the kingdom of God.

xxxii

And when they had sung a hymn, they went out unto the mount of Olives.

And Jesus saith unto them, All ye shall be offended: for it is written, I will smite the shepherd, and the sheep shall be scattered abroad. Howbeit, after I am raised up, I will go before you into Galilee. But Peter said unto him, Although all shall be offended, yet will not I. And Jesus saith unto him, Verily I say unto thee, that thou today, even this night, before the cock crow twice, shalt deny me thrice. But he spake exceeding vehemently, If I must die with thee, I will not deny thee. And in like manner also said they all.

And they come unto a place which was named Gethsemane: and he saith unto his disciples, Sit ye here, while I pray. And he taketh with him Peter and James and John, and began to be greatly amazed, and sore troubled. And he saith unto them, My soul is exceeding sorrowful even unto death: abide ye here, and watch. And he went forward a little, and fell on the ground, and prayed that, if it were possible, the hour might pass away from him. And he said, Abba, Father, all things are possible unto thee; remove this cup from me: howbeit not what I will, but what thou wilt. And he cometh, and findeth them sleeping, and saith unto Peter, Simon, sleepest thou? couldest thou not watch one hour? Watch and pray, that ye enter not into temptation: the spirit indeed is willing, but the flesh is weak. And again he went away, and prayed, saying the same words. And again he came, and found them sleeping, for their eyes were very heavy; and they wist not what to answer him. And he cometh the third time, and saith unto them, Sleep on now, and take your rest: it is enough; the hour is come; behold, the Son of man is betrayed into the hands of sinners. Arise, let us be going: behold, he that betrayeth me is at hand.

And straightway, while he yet spake, cometh Judas, one of the twelve, and with him a multitude with swords and staves, from the chief priests and the scribes and the elders. Now he that betrayed him had given them a token, saying, Whomsoever I shall kiss, that is he; take him, and lead him away safely. And when he was come,

St. Mark xxxii

straightway he came to him, and saith, Rabbi; and kissed him. And they laid hands on him, and took him. But a certain one of them that stood by drew his sword, and smote the servant of the high priest, and struck off his ear. And Jesus answered and said unto them, Are ye come out, as against a robber, with swords and staves to seize me? I was daily with you in the temple teaching, and ye took me not: but this is done that the scriptures might be fulfilled. And they all left him, and fled.

And a certain young man followed with him, having a linen cloth cast about him, over his naked body: and they lay hold on him; but he left the linen cloth, and fled naked.

And they led Jesus away to the high priest: and there come together with him all the chief priests and the elders and the scribes. And Peter had followed him afar off, even within, into the court of the high priest; and he was sitting with the officers, and warming himself in the light of the fire. Now the chief priests and the whole council sought witness against Jesus to put him to death; and found it not. For many bare false witness against him, and their witness agreed not together. And there stood up certain, and bare false witness against him, saying, We heard him say, I will destroy this temple that is made with hands, and in three days I will build another made without hands. And not even so did their witness agree together. And the high priest stood up in the midst, and asked Jesus, saying, Answerest thou nothing? what is it which these witness against thee? But he held his peace, and answered nothing. Again the high priest asked him, and saith unto him, Art thou the Christ, the Son of the Blessed? And Jesus said, I am: and ye shall see the Son of man sitting at the right hand of power, and coming with the clouds of heaven. And the high priest rent his clothes, and saith, What further need have we of witnesses? Ye have heard the blasphemy: what think ye? And they all condemned him to be worthy of death. And some began to spit on him, and to cover his face, and to buffet him, and to say unto him, Prophesy: and the officers received him with blows of their hands.

And as Peter was beneath in the court, there cometh one of the maids of the high priest; and seeing Peter warming himself, she looked upon him, and saith, Thou also wast with the Nazarene, even Jesus. But he denied, saying, I neither know, nor understand what thou sayest: and he went out into the porch; and the cock crew. And the maid saw him, and began again to say to them that stood by, This is one of them. But he again denied it. And after a little while again they that stood by said to Peter, Of a truth thou art one of them; for thou art a Galilæan. But he began to curse and to swear, I know not this man of whom ye speak. And straightway the second time the cock crew. And Peter called to mind the word, how that Jesus said unto him, Before the cock crow twice, thou shalt deny me thrice. And when he thought thereon, he wept.

xxxiii

And straightway in the morning the chief priests with the elders and scribes, and the whole council, held a consultation, and bound Jesus, and carried him away, and delivered him up to Pilate. And Pilate asked him, Art thou the King of the Jews? And he answering saith unto him, Thou sayest. And the chief priests accused him of many things. And Pilate again asked him, saying, Answerest thou nothing? behold how many things they accuse thee of. But Jesus no more answered anything; insomuch that Pilate marvelled.

Now at the feast he used to release unto them one prisoner, whom they asked of him. And there was one called Barabbas, lying bound with them that had made insurrection, men who in the insurrection had committed murder. And the multitude went up and began to ask him to do as he was wont to do unto them. And Pilate answered them, saying, Will ye that I release unto you the King of the Jews? For he perceived that for envy the chief priests had delivered him up. But the chief priests stirred up the multitude, that he should rather release Barabbas unto them. And Pilate again answered and said unto them, What then shall I do unto him whom ye call the King of the Jews? And they cried out again, Crucify him. And Pilate said unto them, Why, what evil hath he done? But they cried out exceedingly, Crucify him. And Pilate, wishing to content the multitude, released unto them Barabbas, and delivered Jesus, when he had scourged him, to be crucified.

xxxiv

And the soldiers led him away within the court, which is the Prætorium; and they call together the whole band. And they clothe him with purple, and plaiting a crown of thorns, they put it on him; and they began to salute him, Hail, King of the Jews! And they smote his head with a reed, and did spit upon him, and bowing their knees worshipped him. And when they had mocked him, they took off from him the purple, and put on him his garments. And they lead him out to crucify him.

And they compel one passing by, Simon of Cyrene, coming from the country, the father of Alexander and Rufus, to go with them, that he might bear his cross. And they bring him unto the place *Golgotha*, which is, being interpreted, The place of a skull. And they offered him wine mingled with myrrh: but he received it not. And they crucify him, and part his garments among them, casting lots upon them, what each should take. And it was the third hour, and they crucified him. And the superscription of his accusation was written over:

The King of the Jews

And with him they crucify two robbers; one on his right hand, and one on his left. And they that passed by railed on him, wagging their heads, and saying, Ha! thou that destroyest the temple, and buildest it in three days, save thyself, and come down from the cross. In like manner also the chief priests mocking him among themselves with the scribes said, He saved others; himself he cannot save. Let the Christ, the King of Israel, now come down from the cross, that we may see and believe. And they that were crucified with him reproached him.

And when the sixth hour was come, there was darkness over the whole land until the ninth hour. And at the ninth hour Jesus cried with a loud voice, *Eloi, Eloi, lama sabachthani?* which is, being interpreted, My God, my God, why hast thou forsaken me? And some of them that stood by, when they heard it, said, Behold, he calleth Elijah. And one ran, and filling a sponge full of vinegar, put it on a reed, and gave him to drink, saying, Let be; let us see whether Elijah cometh to take him down. And Jesus uttered a loud voice, and gave up the ghost. And the veil of the temple was rent in twain from the top to the bottom. And when the centurion, which stood by over against him, saw that he so gave up the ghost, he said, Truly this man was the Son of God. And there were also women beholding from afar: among whom were both

Mary Magdalene, and Mary the mother of James the less and of Joses, and Salome; who, when he was in Galilee, followed him, and ministered unto him; and many other women which came up with him unto Jerusalem.

xxxv

And when even was now come, because it was the Preparation,* there came Joseph of Arimathea, a councillor of honourable estate, who also himself was looking for the kingdom of God; and he boldly went in unto Pilate, and asked for the body of Jesus. And Pilate marvelled if he were already dead: and calling unto him the centurion, he asked him whether he had been any while dead. And when he learned it of the centurion, he granted the corpse to Joseph. And he bought a linen cloth, and taking him down, wound him in the linen cloth, and laid him in a tomb which had been hewn out of a rock; and he rolled a stone against the door of the tomb. And Mary Magdalene and Mary the mother of Joses beheld where he was laid.

xxxvi

And when the sabbath was past, Mary Magdalene, and Mary the mother of James, and Salome, bought spices, that they might come and anoint him. And very early on

* That is, the day before the sabbath.

the first day of the week, they come to the tomb when the sun was risen. And they were saying among themselves, Who shall roll us away the stone from the door of the tomb? and looking up, they see that the stone is rolled back: for it was exceeding great. And entering into the tomb, they saw a young man sitting on the right side, arrayed in a white robe; and they were amazed. And he saith unto them, Be not amazed: ye seek Jesus, the Nazarene, which hath been crucified: he is risen, he is not here: behold, the place where they laid him! But go, tell his disciples and Peter, He goeth before you into Galilee: there shall ye see him, as he said unto you. And they went out, and fled from the tomb; for trembling and astonishment had come upon them: and they said nothing to any one; for they were afraid.

Appendix

Now when he was risen early on the first day of the week, he appeared first to Mary Magdalene, from whom he had cast out seven devils. She went and told them that had been with him, as they mourned and wept. And they, when they heard that he was alive, and had been seen of her, disbelieved.

And after these things he was manifested in another form unto two of them, as they walked, on their way into

Appendix   St. Mark

the country. And they went away, and told it unto the rest: neither believed they them.

And afterward he was manifested unto the eleven themselves as they sat at meat; and he upbraided them with their unbelief and hardness of heart, because they believed not them which had seen him after he was risen. And he said unto them: Go ye into all the world, and preach the gospel to the whole creation. He that believeth and is baptized shall be saved; but he that disbelieveth shall be condemned. And these signs shall follow them that believe: in my name shall they cast out devils; they shall speak with new tongues; they shall take up serpents, and if they drink any deadly thing, it shall in no wise hurt them; they shall lay hands on the sick, and they shall recover.

So then the Lord Jesus, after he had spoken unto them, was received up into heaven, and sat down at the right hand of God. And they went forth, and preached everywhere, the Lord working with them, and confirming the word by the signs that followed.

Amen

An Epistle to Hebrews

I

God, having of old time spoken unto the fathers in the prophets by divers portions and in divers manners, hath at the end of these days spoken unto us in a Son, whom he appointed heir of all things, through whom also he made the worlds; who, being the effulgence of his glory, and the very image of his substance, and upholding all things by the word of his power, when he had made purification of sins, sat down on the right hand of the Majesty on high; having become by so much better than the angels, as he hath inherited a more excellent name than they.

For unto which of the angels said he at any time,

> *Thou art my Son,*
> *This day have I begotten thee?*

and again,

> *I will be to him a Father,*
> *And he shall be to me a son?*

And when he again bringeth in the firstborn into the world he saith, *And let all the angels of God worship him.* And of the angels he saith,

An Epistle

> *Who maketh his angels winds,*
> *And his ministers a flame of fire:*

but of the Son he saith,

> *Thy throne, O God, is for ever and ever;*
> *And the sceptre of uprightness is the sceptre of thy kingdom.*
> *Thou hast loved righteousness, and hated iniquity;*
> *Therefore God, thy God, hath anointed thee*
> *With the oil of gladness above thy fellows.*

And,

> *Thou, Lord, in the beginning hast laid the foundation of the earth,*
> *And the heavens are the works of thy hands:*
> *They shall perish; but thou continuest:*
> *And they all shall wax old as doth a garment;*
> *And as a mantle shalt thou roll them up,*
> *As a garment, and they shall be changed:*
> *But thou art the same,*
> *And thy years shall not fail.*

But of which of the angels hath he said at any time,

> *Sit thou on my right hand,*
> *Till I make thine enemies the footstool of thy feet?*

to Hebrews

Are they not all ministering spirits, sent forth to do service for the sake of them that shall inherit salvation?

Therefore we ought to give the more earnest heed to the things that were heard, lest haply we drift away. For if the word spoken through angels proved stedfast, and every transgression and disobedience received a just recompense of reward; how shall we escape, if we neglect so great salvation? which having at the first been spoken through the Lord, was confirmed unto us by them that heard; God also bearing witness with them, both by signs and wonders, and by manifold powers, and by gifts of the Holy Ghost, according to his own will. For not unto angels did he subject the world to come, whereof we speak. But one hath somewhere testified, saying,

What is man, that thou art mindful of him?
Or the son of man, that thou visitest him?
Thou madest him a little lower than the angels;
Thou crownedst him with glory and honour,
And didst set him over the works of thy hands:
Thou didst put all things in subjection under his feet.

For in that he subjected 'all things' unto him, he left nothing that is not subject to him.

But now we see not yet all things subjected to him. But we behold him who hath been made a little lower than the angels, even Jesus, because of the suffering of death crowned with glory and honour, that by the grace of God he should taste death for every man. For it became him, for whom are all things, and through whom are all things, in bringing many sons unto glory, to make the author of their salvation perfect through sufferings. For both he that sanctifieth and they that are sanctified are all of one: for which cause he is not ashamed to call them brethren, saying,

I will declare thy name unto my brethren,
In the midst of the congregation will I sing thy praise.

And again, *I will put my trust in him.* And again, *Behold, I and the children which God hath given me.* Since then the children are sharers in flesh and blood, he also himself in like manner partook of the same; that through death he might bring to nought him that had the power of death, that is, the devil; and might deliver all them who through fear of death were all their lifetime subject to bondage. For verily not of angels doth he take hold, but he taketh hold of the seed of Abraham. Wherefore it behoved him in all things to be made like unto his brethren, that he might be a merciful and faithful HIGH PRIEST in things pertaining to God, to make propitiation for the sins of the people. For in that he himself hath suffered being tempted, he is able to succour them that are tempted.

II

Wherefore, holy brethren, partakers of a heavenly calling, consider the Apostle and High Priest of our confession, even Jesus; who was faithful to him that appointed him, as also was Moses 'in all His house.' For he hath been counted worthy of more glory than Moses, by so much as he that established the house hath more honour than the house. For every house is established by some one; but he that established all things is God. And Moses indeed was 'faithful in all His house' as a servant, for a testimony of those things which were afterward to be spoken; but Christ as a son, over His house; whose house are we, if we hold fast our boldness and the glorying of our hope firm unto the end. Wherefore, even as the Holy Ghost saith,

> *Today, if ye shall hear his voice,*
> *Harden not your hearts, as in the provocation,*
> *Like as in the day of the temptation in the wilderness,*
> *Where your fathers tempted me by proving me,*
> *And saw my works forty years:*

Wherefore

> *I was displeased with this generation,*
> *And said, they do alway err in their heart;*

An Epistle

But they did not know my ways;
As I sware in my wrath,
They shall not enter into my rest.

Take heed, brethren, lest haply there shall be in any one of you an evil heart of unbelief, in falling away from the living God: but exhort one another day by day, so long as it is called *Today;* lest any one of you be hardened by the deceitfulness of sin: for we are become partakers of Christ, if we hold fast the beginning of our confidence firm unto the end, while it is said,

Today if ye shall hear his voice,
Harden not your hearts, as in the provocation.

For who, when they heard, did provoke? nay, did not all they that came out of Egypt by Moses? And with whom was he displeased forty years? was it not with them that sinned, whose carcases fell in the wilderness? And to whom sware he that they should not enter into his rest, but to them that were disobedient? And we see that they were not able to enter in because of unbelief. Let us fear therefore, lest haply, a promise being left of entering into his rest, any one of you should seem to have come short of it. For indeed we have had good tidings preached unto us, even as also they: but the word of hearing did not profit them, because they were not united by faith with them that heard. For we which have believed do enter into that rest; even as he hath said,

> *As I sware in my wrath,*
> *They shall not enter into my rest:*

although the works were finished from the foundation of the world. For he hath said somewhere of the seventh day on this wise, *And God rested on the seventh day from all his works;* and in this place again,

> *They shall not enter into my rest.*

Seeing therefore it remaineth that some should enter thereinto, and they to whom the good tidings were before preached failed to enter in because of disobedience, he again defineth a certain day, saying in David, after so long a time, *Today,* as it hath been before said,

> *Today if ye shall hear his voice,*
> *Harden not your hearts.*

For if Joshua had given them rest, he would not have spoken afterward of another day. There remaineth therefore a sabbath rest for the people of God. For he that is entered into his rest hath himself also rested from his works, as God did from his. Let us therefore give diligence to enter into that rest, that no man fall after the same example of disobedience. For the word of God is living, and active, and sharper than any two-edged sword, and piercing even to the dividing of soul and spirit, of both joints and marrow, and quick to discern the thoughts and intents of the heart. And there is no creature that is not manifest in his sight: but all things are naked and laid open before the eyes of him with whom we have to do.

Having then a great high priest, who hath passed through the heavens, Jesus the Son of God, let us hold fast our confession. For we have not a high priest that cannot be touched with the feeling of our infirmities; but one that hath been in all points tempted like as we are, yet without sin. Let us therefore draw near with boldness unto the throne of grace, that we may receive mercy, and may find grace to help us in time of need. For every high priest, being taken from among men, is appointed for men in things pertaining to God, that he may offer both gifts and sacrifices for sins: who can bear gently with the ignorant and erring, for that he himself also is compassed with infirmity; and by reason thereof is bound, as for the people, so also for himself, to offer for sins. And no man taketh the honour unto himself, but when he is called of God, even as was Aaron. So Christ also glorified not himself to be made a high priest, but he that spake unto him,

Thou art my Son,
This day have I begotten thee:

to Hebrews

as he saith also in another place,

> *Thou art a priest for ever
> After the order of Melchizedek.*

Who in the days of his flesh, having offered up prayers and supplications with strong crying and tears unto him that was able to save him out of death, and having been heard for his godly fear, though he was a Son, yet learned obedience by the things which he suffered; and having been made perfect, he became unto all them that obey him the author of eternal salvation; named of God A HIGH PRIEST AFTER THE ORDER OF MELCHIZEDEK.

Of which we have many things to say, and hard of interpretation, seeing ye are become dull of hearing. For when by reason of the time ye ought to be teachers, ye have need again that some one teach you the rudiments of the first principles of the oracles of God; and are become such as have need of milk, and not of solid food. For every one that partaketh of milk is without experience of the word of righteousness; for he is a babe. But solid food is for fullgrown men, even those who by reason of use have their senses exercised to discern good and evil. Wherefore let us cease to speak of the first principles of Christ, and press on unto full growth; not laying again a foundation — of repentance from dead works, and of faith toward God, of the teaching of baptisms and of laying on of hands, and of resurrection of the dead, and of eternal judgement. And this will we do, if God permit. For as touching those who were once enlightened and tasted of the heavenly gift, and were made partakers of the Holy Ghost, and tasted the word of God that it is good, and the powers of the age to come, and then fell away, it is impossible to renew them again unto repentance; the while they crucify to themselves the Son of God afresh, and put him to an open shame. For the land which hath drunk the rain that cometh oft upon it, and bringeth forth herbs meet for them for whose sake it is also tilled, receiveth blessing from God: but if it beareth thorns and thistles, it is rejected and nigh unto a curse; whose end is to be burned. But, beloved, we are persuaded better things of you, and things that accompany salvation, though we thus speak: for God is not unrighteous to forget your work and the love which ye shewed toward his name, in that ye ministered unto the saints, and still do minister. And we desire that each one of you may shew the same diligence unto the fulness of hope even to the end: that ye be not sluggish, but imitators of them who through faith and patience inherit the promises. For when God made promise to Abraham, since he could swear by none greater, he sware by himself, saying, Surely blessing I will bless thee, and multiplying I will multiply thee. And thus, having patiently endured, he obtained the promise. For men swear by the greater:

to Hebrews

and in every dispute of theirs the oath is final for confirmation. Wherein God, being minded to shew more abundantly unto the heirs of the promise the immutability of his counsel, interposed with an oath: that by two immutable things, in which it is impossible for God to lie, we may have a strong encouragement, who have fled for refuge to lay hold of the hope set before us; which we have as an anchor of the soul, a hope both sure and stedfast and entering into that which is within the veil; whither as a forerunner Jesus entered for us, having become a high priest for ever after the order of Melchizedek.

For this Melchizedek, king of Salem, priest of God Most High, who met Abraham returning from the slaughter of the kings, and blessed him, to whom also Abraham divided a tenth part of all — being first, by interpretation, 'King of righteousness,' and then also 'King of Salem,' which is, 'King of peace'; without father, without mother, without genealogy, having neither beginning of days nor end of life, but made like unto the Son of God — ABIDETH A PRIEST CONTINUALLY. Now consider how great this man was, unto whom Abraham, the patriarch, gave a tenth out of the chief spoils. And they indeed of the sons of Levi that receive the priest's office have commandment to take tithes of the people according to the law, that is, of their brethren, though these have come out of the loins of Abraham: but he whose genealogy is not counted from them hath taken tithes of Abraham, and hath blessed him that hath the promises: but without any dispute the less is blessed of the better. And here men that die receive tithes; but there one, of whom it is witnessed that he liveth. And, so to say, through Abraham even Levi, who receiveth tithes, hath paid tithes; for he was yet in the loins of his father, when Melchizedek met him. Now if there was perfection through the Levitical priesthood (for under it hath the people received the law), what further need was there that another priest should arise after the order of Melchizedek, and not be reckoned after the order of Aaron? For the priesthood being changed, there is made of necessity a change also of the law. For he of whom these things are said belongeth to another tribe, from which no man hath given attendance at the altar: for it is evident that our Lord hath sprung out of Judah, as to which tribe Moses spake nothing concerning priests. And what we say is yet more abundantly evident, if after the likeness of Melchizedek there ariseth another priest, who hath been made, not after the law of a carnal commandment, but after the power of an endless life: for it is witnessed of him,

> *Thou art a priest for ever*
> *After the order of Melchizedek.*

For there is a disannulling of a foregoing commandment because of its weakness and unprofitableness (for the law made nothing perfect), and a bringing in thereupon of a better hope, through which we draw nigh unto God. And inasmuch as it is not without the taking of an oath — for they indeed have been made priests without an oath; but he with an oath by him that saith of him,

The Lord sware and will not repent himself,
Thou art a priest for ever —

by so much also hath Jesus become the surety of a better covenant. And they indeed have been made priests many in number, because that by death they are hindered from continuing: but he, because he abideth for ever, hath his priesthood unchangeable. Wherefore also he is able to save to the uttermost them that draw near unto God through him, seeing he ever liveth to make intercession for them. For such a high priest became us, holy, guileless, undefiled, separated from sinners, and made higher than the heavens; who needeth not daily, like those high priests, to offer up sacrifices, first for his own sins, and then for the sins of the people: for this he did once for all, when he offered up himself. For the law appointeth men high priests, having infirmity; but the word of the oath, which was after the law, appointeth a Son, perfected for evermore.

Now in the things which we are saying the chief point is this: We have such a high priest, who sat down on the right hand of the throne of the Majesty in the heavens, a

→**An Epistle**

minister of the sanctuary, and of the TRUE TABERNACLE, which the Lord pitched, not man. For every high priest is appointed to offer both gifts and sacrifices: wherefore it is necessary that this high priest also have somewhat to offer. Now if he were on earth, he would not be a priest at all, seeing there are those who offer the gifts according to the law; who serve that which is a copy and shadow of the heavenly things, even as Moses is warned of God when he is about to make the tabernacle: for, See, saith he, that thou make all things according to the pattern that was shewed thee in the mount. But now hath he obtained a ministry the more excellent, by how much also he is the mediator of a better covenant, which hath been enacted upon better promises.* Now even the first covenant had ordi-

---

* For if that first covenant had been faultless, then would no place have been sought for a second. For finding fault with them, he saith, *Behold, the days come, saith the Lord, that I will make a new covenant with the house of Israel and with the house of Judah; not according to the covenant that I made with their fathers in the day that I took them by the hand to lead them forth out of the land of Egypt; for they continued not in my covenant, and I regarded them not, saith the Lord. For this is the covenant that I will make with the house of Israel after those days, saith the Lord; I will put my laws into their mind, and on their heart also will I write them: and I will be to them a God, and they shall be to me a people: and they shall not teach every man his fellow-citizen, and every man his brother, saying, Know the Lord: for all shall know me, from the least to the greatest of them. For I will be merciful to their iniquities, and their sins I will remember no more.* In that he saith, *A new covenant*, he hath made the first old. But that which is becoming old and waxeth aged is nigh unto vanishing away.

nances of divine service, and its sanctuary, a sanctuary of this world. For there was a tabernacle prepared, the first, wherein were the candlestick, and the table, and the shewbread; which is called the Holy place. And after the second veil, the tabernacle which is called the Holy of holies; having a golden censer, and the ark of the covenant overlaid round about with gold, wherein is a golden pot holding the manna, and Aaron's rod that budded, and the tables of the covenant; and above it cherubim of glory overshadowing the mercy-seat; of which things we cannot now speak severally. Now these things having been thus prepared, the priests go in continually into the first tabernacle, accomplishing the services; but into the second the high priest alone, once in the year, not without blood, which he offereth for himself, and for the errors of the people: the Holy Ghost this signifying, that the way into the holy place hath not yet been made manifest, while as the first tabernacle is yet standing. Which is a parable for the time now present: according to which are offered both gifts and sacrifices that cannot, as touching the conscience, make the worshipper perfect, being only (with meats and drinks and divers washings) carnal ordinances, imposed until a time of reformation. But Christ having come a high priest of the good things to come, through the greater and more perfect tabernacle, not made with hands, that is to say, not of this creation, nor yet through the blood of goats and calves, but through his own blood, entered in once for all into the holy place, having obtained eternal redemption.

For if the blood of goats and bulls, and the ashes of a heifer sprinkling them that have been defiled, sanctify unto the cleanness of the flesh: how much more shall the blood of Christ, who through the eternal spirit offered himself without blemish unto God, cleanse your conscience from dead works to serve the living God? And for this cause he is the MEDIATOR OF A NEW COVENANT, that a death having taken place for the redemption of the transgressions that were under the first covenant, they that have been called may receive the promise of the eternal inheritance. For where a covenant is, there must of necessity be the death of him that made it. For a covenant is of force where there hath been death: for doth it ever avail while he that made it liveth? Wherefore even the first covenant hath not been dedicated without blood. For when every commandment had been spoken by Moses unto all the people according to the law, he took the blood of the calves and the goats, with water and scarlet wool and hyssop, and sprinkled both the book itself, and all the people, saying, This is the blood of the covenant which God commanded to you-ward. Moreover the tabernacle and all the vessels of the ministry he sprinkled in like manner with the blood. And according to the law, I may almost say, all things are cleansed with blood, and apart from shedding of blood there is no remission. It was

to Hebrews

necessary therefore that the copies of the things in the heavens should be cleansed with these; but the heavenly things themselves with better sacrifices than these. For Christ entered not into a holy place made with hands, like in pattern to the true: but into heaven itself, now to appear before the face of God for us: nor yet that he should offer himself often; as the high priest entereth into the holy place year by year with blood not his own; else must he often have suffered since the foundation of the world: but now once at the end of the ages hath he been manifested to put away sin by the sacrifice of himself. And inasmuch as it is appointed unto men once to die, and after this cometh judgement; so Christ also, having been once offered 'to bear the sins of many,' shall appear a second time, apart from sin, to them that wait for him, unto salvation. For the law having a shadow of the good things to come, not the very image of the things, they can never with the same sacrifices year by year, which they offer continually, make perfect them that draw nigh. Else would they not have ceased to be offered, because the worshippers, having been once cleansed, would have had no more conscience of sins? But in those sacrifices there is a remembrance made of sins year by year. For it is impossible that the blood of bulls and goats should take away sins. Wherefore when he cometh into the world, he saith,

⇥ An Epistle

Sacrifice and offering thou wouldest not,
But a body didst thou prepare for me;
In whole burnt offerings and sacrifices for sin thou hadst
　no pleasure:
Then said I, Lo, I am come
(In the roll of the book it is written of me)
To do thy will, O God.

Saying above, *Sacrifices and offerings and whole burnt offerings and sacrifices for sin thou wouldest not, neither hadst pleasure therein* (the which are offered according to the law), then hath he said, *Lo, I am come to do thy will.* He taketh away the first, that he may establish the second. In which 'will' we have been sanctified through the offering of the body of Jesus Christ once for all. And every priest indeed standeth day by day ministering and offering oftentimes the same sacrifices, the which can never take away sins: but he, when he had offered one sacrifice for sins for ever, sat down on the right hand of God; from henceforth expecting till his enemies be made the footstool of his feet. For by one offering he hath perfected for ever them that are sanctified. And the Holy Ghost also beareth witness to us: for after he hath said, *This is the covenant that I will make with them after those days, saith the Lord; I will put my laws on their heart, and upon their mind also will I write them;* then saith he, *And their sins and their iniquities will I remember no more.* Now where remission of these is, there is no more offering for sin.

III

Having therefore, brethren, boldness to enter into the holy place by the blood of Jesus, by the way which he dedicated for us, a new and living way, through the veil, that is to say, his flesh; and having a great priest over the house of God; let us draw near with a true heart in fulness of faith, having our hearts sprinkled from an evil conscience, and our body washed with pure water: let us hold fast the confession of our hope that it waver not; for he is faithful that promised: and let us consider one another to provoke unto love and good works; not forsaking the assembling of ourselves together, as the custom of some is, but exhorting one another. And so much the more, as ye see the day drawing nigh. For if we sin wilfully after that we have received the knowledge of the truth, there remaineth no more a sacrifice for sins, but a certain fearful expectation of judgement, and a jealousy of fire which shall devour the adversaries. A man that hath set at nought Moses' law dieth without compassion on the word of two or three witnesses: of how much sorer punishment, think ye, shall he be judged worthy, who hath trodden under foot the Son of God, and hath counted the blood of the covenant, wherewith he was sanctified, an unholy thing, and hath done despite unto the Spirit of grace? For we know him that said, *Vengeance belongeth unto me, I will recompense.* And again, *The Lord shall judge his people.* It is a fearful thing to fall into the hands of the living God. But call to remembrance the former days, in which, after ye were enlightened, ye endured a great conflict of sufferings; partly, being made a gazing-stock both by reproaches and afflictions; and partly, becoming partakers with them that were so used. For ye both had compassion on them that were in bonds, and took joyfully the spoiling of your possessions, knowing that ye have your own selves for a better possession and an abiding one. Cast not away therefore your boldness, which hath great recompense of reward. For ye have need of patience, that, having done the will of God, ye may receive the promise. *For yet a very little while, he that cometh shall come, and shall not tarry. But my righteous one shall live BY FAITH: and if he shrink back, my soul hath no pleasure in him.* But we are not of them that shrink back unto perdition; but of them that have faith unto the saving of the soul.

Now faith is the giving substance to things hoped for, the proving of things not seen. For therein the elders had witness borne to them. By faith we understand that the worlds have been framed by the word of God, so that what is seen hath not been made out of things which do appear. By faith Abel offered unto God a more excellent sacrifice than Cain, through which he had witness borne to him that he was righteous, God bearing witness in re-

to Hebrews

spect of his gifts: and through it he being dead yet speaketh. By faith Enoch was translated that he should not see death; and he was not found, because God translated him: for before his translation he hath had witness borne to him that he had been well-pleasing unto God: and without faith it is impossible to be well-pleasing unto him: for he that cometh to God must believe that he is, and that he is a rewarder of them that seek after him. By faith Noah, being warned of God concerning things not seen as yet, moved with godly fear, prepared an ark to the saving of his house; through which he condemned the world, and became heir of the righteousness which is according to faith. By faith Abraham, when he was called, obeyed to go out unto a place which he was to receive for an inheritance; and he went out, not knowing whither he went. By faith he became a sojourner in the land of promise, as in a land not his own, dwelling in tents, with Isaac and Jacob, the heirs with him of the same promise: for he looked for the city which hath the foundations, whose architect and maker is God. By faith even Sarah herself received power to conceive seed when she was past age, since she counted him faithful who had promised: wherefore also there sprang of one, and him as good as dead, so many as the stars of heaven in multitude, and as the sand, which is by the sea shore, innumerable. These all died in faith, not having received the promises, but having seen them and greeted them from afar, and having confessed that they were strangers and pilgrims on the earth. For they that say such things make it manifest that they are seeking after a country of their own. And if indeed they had been mindful of that country from which they went out, they would have had opportunity to return. But now they desire a better country, that is, a heavenly: wherefore God is not ashamed of them, to be called their God: for he hath prepared for them a city. By faith Abraham, being tried, offered up Isaac: yea, he that had gladly received the promises was offering up his only begotten son; even he to whom it was said, *In Isaac shall thy seed be called:* accounting that God is able to raise up, even from the dead; from whence he did also in a parable receive him back. By faith Isaac blessed Jacob and Esau, even concerning things to come. By faith Jacob, when he was a dying, blessed each of the sons of Joseph; and worshipped, leaning upon the top of his staff. By faith Joseph, when his end was nigh, made mention of the departure of the children of Israel; and gave commandment concerning his bones. By faith Moses, when he was born, was hid three months by his parents, because they saw he was a goodly child; and they were not afraid of the king's commandment. By faith Moses, when he was grown up, refused to be called the son of Pharaoh's daughter; choosing rather to be evil entreated with the people of God, than to enjoy the pleasures of sin for a season; accounting the reproach of the Christ greater riches than the treasures of

to Hebrews

Egypt: for he looked unto the recompense of reward. By faith he forsook Egypt, not fearing the wrath of the king: for he endured, as seeing him who is invisible. By faith he kept the passover, and the sprinkling of the blood, that the destroyer of the firstborn should not touch them. By faith they passed through the Red sea as by dry land: which the Egyptians assaying to do were swallowed up. By faith the walls of Jericho fell down, after they had been compassed about for seven days. By faith Rahab the harlot perished not with them that were disobedient, having received the spies with peace. And what shall I more say? for the time will fail me if I tell of Gideon, Barak, Samson, Jephthah; of David and Samuel and the prophets: who through faith subdued kingdoms, wrought righteousness, obtained promises, stopped the mouths of lions, quenched the power of fire, escaped the edge of the sword, from weakness were made strong, waxed mighty in war, turned to flight armies of aliens. Women received their dead by a resurrection: and others were tortured, not accepting their deliverance; that they might obtain a better resurrection: and others had trial of mockings and scourgings, yea, moreover of bonds and imprisonment: they were stoned, they were sawn asunder, they were tempted, they were slain with the sword: they went about in sheepskins, in goatskins; being destitute, afflicted, evil entreated (of whom the world was not worthy), wandering in deserts and mountains and caves, and the holes of the earth. And these all, having had witness borne to them through their faith, received not the promise, God having provided some better thing concerning us, that apart from us they should not be made perfect.

Therefore let us also, seeing we are compassed about with so great a cloud of witnesses, lay aside all cumbrance and the sin which is admired of many, and let us run with patience the race that is set before us, looking unto Jesus the author and perfecter of our faith, who for the joy that was set before him endured the cross, despising shame, and hath sat down at the right hand of the throne of God. For consider him that hath endured such gainsaying of sinners against themselves, that ye wax not weary, fainting in your souls. Ye have not yet resisted unto blood, striving against sin: and ye have forgotten the exhortation, which reasoneth with you as with sons,

My son, regard not lightly the chastening of the Lord,
Nor faint when thou art reproved of him;
For whom the Lord loveth he chasteneth,
And scourgeth every son whom he receiveth.

Endure unto chastening: God dealeth with you as with sons; for what son is there whom his father chasteneth not? But if ye are without chastening, whereof all have been made partakers, then are ye bastards, and not sons. Furthermore, we had the fathers of our flesh to chasten us,

to Hebrews

and we gave them reverence: shall we not much rather be in subjection unto the Father of spirits, and live? For they verily for a few days chastened us as seemed good to them; but he for our profit, that we may be partakers of his holiness. All chastening seemeth for the present to be not joyous, but grievous: yet afterward it yieldeth peaceable fruit unto them that have been exercised thereby, even the fruit of righteousness. Wherefore lift up the hands that hang down, and the palsied knees; and make straight paths for your feet, that that which is lame be not put out of joint, but rather be healed. Follow after peace with all men, and the sanctification without which no man shall see the Lord: looking carefully whether there be any man that falleth short of the grace of God; lest any root of bitterness springing up trouble you, and thereby the many be defiled; whether there be any fornicator, or profane person, as Esau, who for one mess of meat sold his own birthright: for ye know that even when he afterward desired to inherit the blessing, he was rejected (for he found no place of repentance), though he sought it diligently with tears.

For ye are not come unto a palpable and kindled fire, and unto blackness, and darkness, and tempest, and the sound of a trumpet, and the voice of words; which voice they that heard intreated that no word more should be spoken unto them: for they could not endure that which was enjoined, If even a beast touch the mountain, it shall be stoned; and (so fearful was the appearance), Moses said, I exceedingly fear and quake: but ye are come unto mount Zion, and unto the city of the living God, the heavenly Jerusalem, and to innumerable hosts of angels, to the general assembly and church of the firstborn who are enrolled in heaven, and to God the Judge of all, and to the spirits of just men made perfect, and to Jesus the mediator of a new covenant, and to the blood of sprinkling that speaketh better than Abel. See that ye refuse not him that speaketh: for if they escaped not, when they refused him that warned them on earth, much more shall not we escape, who turn away from him that warneth from heaven. Whose voice then shook the earth; but now he hath promised, saying, *Yet once more will I make to tremble not the earth only, but also the heaven*: and this word, *Yet once more*, signifieth the removing of those things that are shaken, as of things that have been made, that those things which are not shaken may remain. Wherefore, receiving a kingdom that cannot be shaken, let us have grace, whereby we may offer service well-pleasing to God with reverence and awe: for our God is a consuming fire.

IV

Let love of the brethren continue. Forget not to shew love unto strangers: for thereby some have entertained angels unawares. Remember them that are in bonds, as bound with them; them that are evil entreated, as being yourselves also in the body. Let marriage be had in honour among all, and let the bed be undefiled: for fornicators and adulterers God will judge. Be ye free from the love of money; content with such things as ye have: for himself hath said, I will in no wise fail thee, neither will I in any wise forsake thee. So that with good courage we say,

> *The Lord is my helper; I will not fear:*
> *What shall man do unto me?*

Remember them that had the rule over you, which spake unto you the word of God; and considering the issue of their life, imitate their faith. Jesus Christ is the same yesterday and today, yea and for ever. Be not carried away by divers and strange teachings: for it is good that the heart be stablished by grace; not by meats, wherein they that occupied themselves were not profited. We have an altar, whereof they have no right to eat which serve the tabernacle. For the bodies of those beasts, whose blood is brought into the holy place by the high priest as an offering for sin, are burned without the camp. Wherefore Jesus also, that he might sanctify the people through his own blood, suffered without the gate. Let us therefore go forth unto him without the camp, bearing his reproach. For we have not here an abiding city, but we seek after the city which is to come.

An Epistle to Hebrews

Through him then let us offer up a sacrifice of praise to God continually, that is, the fruit of lips which make confession to his name. But to do good and to communicate forget not: for with such sacrifices God is well pleased. Obey them that have the rule over you, and submit to them: for they watch in behalf of your souls, as they that shall give account; that they may do this with joy, and not with grief: for this were unprofitable for you.

Pray for us: for we are persuaded that we have a good conscience, desiring to live honestly in all things. And I exhort you the more exceedingly to do this, that I may be restored to you the sooner.

Now the God of peace, who brought again from the dead the great shepherd of the sheep with the blood of the eternal covenant, even our Lord Jesus, make you perfect in every good thing to do his will, working in us that which is well-pleasing in his sight, through Jesus Christ; to whom be the glory for ever and ever. Amen.

*

But I exhort you, brethren, bear with the word of exhortation: for I have written unto you in a few words. Know ye that our brother Timothy hath been set at liberty; with whom, if he come shortly, I will see you.

Salute all them that have rule over you, and all the saints. They of Italy salute you.

Grace be with you all. Amen.

The Wisdom

of

St. James

An Epistle

JAMES
*A Servant of God and of the
Lord Jesus Christ*

*To the Twelve Tribes which
are of the DISPERSION:*

Greeting.

i

The Joy of Temptation

A Paradox

Count it all joy, my brethren, *when ye fall into manifold temptations;* knowing that the proof of your faith worketh patience. And let patience have its perfect work, that ye may be perfect and entire, lacking in nothing.

ii

The Prayer for Wisdom

A Maxim

But *if any of you lacketh wisdom, let him ask of God,* who giveth to all liberally and upbraideth not; and it shall be given him. But let him ask in faith, nothing doubting: for he that doubteth is like the surge of the sea driven by the wind and tossed. For let not that man think that he shall receive anything of the Lord; a double-minded man, unstable in all his ways.

iii

A Paradox of High and Low

But *let the brother of low degree glory in his high estate: and the rich, in that he is made low:* because as the flower of the grass he shall pass away. For the sun ariseth with the scorching wind, and withereth the grass; and the flower thereof falleth, and the grace of the fashion of it perisheth: so also shall the rich man fade away in his goings.

iv

On the Sources of the Evil and the Good in us

An Essay

Blessed is the man that endureth temptation: for when he hath been approved, he shall receive the crown of life, which the Lord promised to them that love him. Let no man say when he is tempted, I am tempted of God: for God cannot be tempted with evil, and he himself tempteth no man: but each man is tempted, when he is drawn away by his own lust, and enticed. Then the lust, when it hath conceived, beareth sin: and the sin, when it is fullgrown, bringeth forth death. Be not deceived, my beloved brethren.

Every good gift and every perfect boon is from above, coming down from the Father of lights, with whom can be no variation, neither shadow that is cast by turning. Of his own will he brought us forth by the word of truth, that we should be a kind of firstfruits of his creatures. Know ye this, my beloved brethren. But let every man be swift to hear, slow to speak, slow to wrath: for the wrath of man worketh not the righteousness of God. Wherefore putting away all filthiness and overflowing of wickedness, receive with meekness the inborn word, which is able to save your souls. But be ye doers of the word, and not hearers only, deluding your own selves. For if any one is a hearer of the word, and not a doer, he is like unto a man beholding his natural face in a mirror: for he beholdeth himself, and goeth away, and straightway forgetteth what manner of man he was. But he that looketh into the perfect law, the law of liberty, and so continueth, being not a hearer that forgetteth, but a doer that worketh, this man shall be blessed in his doing. If any man thinketh himself to be religious, while he bridleth not his tongue but deceiveth his heart, this man's religion is vain. Pure religion and undefiled before our God and Father is this, to visit the fatherless and widows in their affliction, and to keep himself unspotted from the world.

V

On Respect of Persons

An Essay

My brethren, hold not the faith of our Lord Jesus Christ, the Lord of glory, with respect of persons. For if there come into your synagogue a man with a gold ring, in fine clothing, and there come in also a poor man in vile clothing; and ye have regard to him that weareth the fine clothing, and say, Sit thou here in a good place; and ye say to the poor man, Stand thou there, or sit under my footstool; do ye not make distinctions among yourselves, and become judges with evil thoughts? Hearken, my beloved brethren; did not God choose them that are poor as to the world to be rich in faith, and heirs of the kingdom which he promised to them that love him? But ye have dishonoured the poor man. Do not the rich oppress you, and themselves drag you before the judgement-seats? Do not they blaspheme the honourable name by the which ye are called? Howbeit if ye fulfil the royal law, according to the scripture, Thou shalt love thy neighbour as thyself, ye do well: but if ye have respect of persons, ye commit sin, being convicted by the law as transgressors. For whosoever shall keep the whole law, and yet stumble in one point, he is become guilty of all. For he that said, Do not commit adultery, said also, Do not kill. Now if thou dost not commit adultery, but killest, thou art become a transgressor of the law. So speak ye, and so do, as men that are to be judged by a law of liberty. For judgement is without mercy to him that hath shewed no mercy: mercy glorieth against judgement.

vi

• Faith and Works

An Essay

What doth it profit, my brethren, if a man say he hath faith, but have not works? can that faith save him? If a brother or sister be naked, and in lack of daily food, and one of you say unto them, Go in peace, be ye warmed and filled; and yet ye give them not the things needful to the body; what doth it profit? Even so faith, if it have not works, is dead in itself. Yea, a man will say, Thou hast faith, and I have works: shew me thy faith apart from thy works, and I by my works will shew thee my faith. Thou believest that God is one; thou doest well: the devils also believe, and shudder. But wilt thou know, O vain man, that faith apart from works is barren? Was not Abraham our father justified by works, in that he offered up Isaac his son upon the altar? Thou seest that faith wrought with his works, and by works was faith made perfect; and the scripture was fulfilled which saith, *And Abraham believed God, and it was reckoned unto him for righteousness;* and he was called the friend of God. Ye see that by works a man is justified, and not only by faith. And in like manner was not also Rahab the harlot justified by works, in that she received the messengers, and sent them out another way? For as the body apart from the spirit is dead, even so faith apart from works is dead.

vii

The Responsibility of Speech

An Essay

Be not many teachers, my brethren, knowing that we shall receive heavier judgement. For in many things we all stumble. If any stumbleth not in word, the same is a perfect man, able to bridle the whole body also. Now if we put the horses' bridles into their mouths, that they may obey us, we turn about their whole body also. Behold, the ships also, though they are so great, and are driven by rough winds, are yet turned about by a very small rudder, whither the impulse of the steersman willeth. So the tongue also is a little member, and boasteth great things. Behold, how much wood is kindled by how small a fire! And the tongue is a fire: the world of iniquity among our members is the tongue, which defileth the whole body, and setteth on fire the wheel of nature, and is set on fire by hell. For every kind of beasts and birds, of creeping things and things in the sea, is tamed, and hath been tamed by mankind: but the tongue can no man tame; it is a restless evil, it is full of deadly poison. Therewith bless we the Lord and Father; and therewith curse we men, which are made after the likeness of God: out of the same mouth cometh forth blessing and cursing. My brethren, these things ought not so to be. Doth the fountain send forth from the same opening sweet water and bitter? can a fig tree, my brethren, yield olives, or a vine figs? neither can salt water yield sweet.

viii

The Earthly Wisdom and the Wisdom from Above

An Essay

Who is wise and understanding among you? let him shew by his good life his works in meekness of wisdom. But if ye have bitter jealousy and faction in your heart, glory not and lie not against the truth. This wisdom is not a wisdom that cometh down from above, but is earthly, sensual, devilish. For where jealousy and faction are, there is confusion and every vile deed. But the wisdom that is from above is first pure, then peaceable, gentle, easy to be intreated, full of mercy and good fruits, without variance, without hypocrisy. And the fruit of righteousness is sown in peace for them that make peace.

ix

On Worldly Pleasures

A Discourse

Whence come wars and whence come fightings among you? come they not hence, even of your pleasures that war in your members? Ye lust, and have not: ye kill, and covet, and cannot obtain: ye fight and war; ye have not, because ye ask not. Ye ask, and receive not, because ye ask amiss, that ye may spend it in your pleasures. Ye adulteresses, know ye not that the friendship of the world is enmity with God? Whosoever therefore would be a friend of the world maketh himself an enemy of God. Or think ye that the scripture speaketh in vain? Doth the spirit which he made to dwell in us long unto envying? But he giveth more grace. Wherefore the scripture saith,

God resisteth the proud, but giveth grace to the humble. Be subject therefore unto God; but resist the devil, and he will flee from you. Draw nigh to God, and he will draw nigh to you. Cleanse your hands, ye sinners; and purify your hearts, ye doubleminded. Be afflicted, and mourn, and weep: let your laughter be turned to mourning, and your joy to heaviness. Humble yourselves in the sight of the Lord, and he shall exalt you.

X

A Maxim against Judging

Speak not one against another, brethren. *He that speaketh against a brother*, or judgeth his brother, *speaketh against the law*, and judgeth the law: but if thou judgest the law, thou art not a doer of the law, but a judge. One only is the lawgiver and judge, even he who is able to save and to destroy: but who art thou that judgest thy neighbour?

xi

The Judgment to Come

A Discourse

Go to now, ye that say, Today or tomorrow we will go into this city, and spend a year there, and trade, and get gain: whereas ye know not what shall be on the morrow. What is your life? For ye are a vapour, that appeareth for a little time, and then vanisheth away. For that ye ought to say, If the Lord will, we shall both live, and do this or that. But now ye glory in your vauntings: all such glorying is evil. To him therefore that knoweth to do good, and doeth it not, to him it is sin.

Go to now, ye rich, weep and howl for your miseries that are coming upon you. Your riches are corrupted, and your garments are moth-eaten. Your gold and your silver are rusted; and their rust shall be for a testimony against you, and shall eat your flesh as fire. Ye have laid up your treasure in the last days. Behold, the hire of the labourers who mowed your fields, which is of you kept back by fraud, crieth out: and the cries of them that reaped have entered into the ears of the Lord of Sabaoth. Ye have lived delicately on the earth, and taken your pleasure; ye have nourished your hearts in a day of slaughter. Ye have condemned, ye have killed the righteous one; he doth not resist you.

Be patient therefore, brethren, until the coming of the Lord. Behold, the husbandman waiteth for the precious fruit of the earth, being patient over it, until it receive the early and latter rain. Be ye also patient; stablish your hearts: for the coming of the Lord is at hand. Murmur not, brethren, one against another, that ye be not judged: behold, the judge standeth before the doors. Take, brethren, for an example of suffering and of patience, the prophets who spake in the name of the Lord. Behold, we call them blessed which endured: ye have heard of the patience of Job, and have seen the end of the Lord, how that the Lord is full of pity, and merciful.

But above all things, my brethren, swear not, neither by the heaven, nor by the earth, nor by any other oath: but let your yea be yea, and your nay, nay; that ye fall not under judgement.

Is any among you suffering? let him pray. Is any cheerful? let him sing praise. Is any among you sick? let him call for the elders of the church; and let them pray over him, anointing him with oil in the name of the Lord: and the prayer of faith shall save him that is sick, and the Lord shall raise him up; and if he have committed sins, it shall be forgiven him. Confess therefore your sins one to another, and pray one for another, that ye may be healed. The supplication of a righteous man availeth much in its working. Elijah was a man of like passions with us, and he prayed fervently that it might not rain; and it rained not on the earth for three years and six months. And he prayed again; and the heaven gave rain, and the earth brought forth her fruit.

xii

The Blessed Work of Converting

A Maxim

My brethren, if any among you do err from the truth, and one convert him; let him know, that *he which converteth a sinner from the error of his way shall save a soul from death, and shall cover a multitude of sins.*

The Epistles General

of

St. Peter

No. I

Peter
An Apostle of Jesus Christ

> *To the Elect who are sojourners of the DISPERSION in Pontus, Galatia, Cappadocia, Asia, and Bithynia: According to the foreknowledge of God the Father, in sanctification of the Spirit, unto obedience and sprinkling of the blood of Jesus Christ:*

*Grace to you and
Peace be multiplied.*

1

BLESSED be the God and Father of our Lord Jesus Christ, who according to his great mercy begat us again unto a living hope by the resurrection of Jesus Christ from the dead, unto an inheritance incorruptible, and undefiled, and that fadeth not away, reserved in heaven for you, who by the power of God are guarded through faith unto a salvation ready to be revealed in the last time. Wherein ye greatly rejoice, though now for a little while, if need be, ye have been put to grief in manifold temptations, that the proof of your faith, being more precious than gold that perisheth though it is proved by fire, might be found unto praise and glory and honour at the revelation of Jesus Christ: whom not having seen ye love; on whom, though now ye see him not, yet believing, ye rejoice greatly with joy unspeakable and full of glory: receiving the end of your faith, even the salvation of your souls. Concerning which salvation the prophets sought and searched diligently, who prophesied of the grace that should come unto you: searching what time or what manner of time the Spirit of Christ which was in them did point unto, when it testified beforehand the sufferings of Christ, and the glories that should follow them. To whom it was revealed, that not unto themselves, but unto you, did they minister these things, which now have been announced unto you through them that preached the gospel unto you by the Holy Ghost sent forth from heaven; which things angels desire to look into.

Wherefore girding up the loins of your mind, be sober and set your hope perfectly on the grace that is to be brought unto you at the revelation of Jesus Christ; as children of obedience, not fashioning yourselves according to your former lusts in the time of your ignorance: but like as he which called you is holy, be ye yourselves also holy in all manner of living; because it is written, *Ye shall be holy; for I am holy*. And if ye call on him as

St. Peter

Father, who without respect of persons judgeth according to each man's work, pass the time of your sojourning in fear: knowing that ye were redeemed, not with corruptible things, with silver or gold, from your vain manner of life handed down from your fathers; but with precious blood, as of a lamb without blemish and without spot, even the blood of Christ: who was foreknown indeed before the foundation of the world, but was manifested at the end of the times for your sake, who through him are believers in God, which raised him from the dead, and gave him glory; so that your faith and hope might be in God. Seeing ye have purified your souls in your obedience to the truth unto unfeigned love of the brethren, love one another from the heart fervently. Having been begotten again, not of corruptible seed, but of incorruptible, through the word of God, which liveth and abideth: — for,

All flesh is as grass,
And all the glory thereof as the flower of grass;
The grass withereth, and the flower falleth,
But the word of the Lord abideth for ever:

and this is the word of good tidings which was preached unto you: — putting away therefore all wickedness, and all guile, and hypocrisies, and envies, and all evil speakings, as newborn babes, long for the spiritual milk which is without guile, that ye may grow thereby unto salvation; if ye have tasted that the Lord is gracious: unto whom coming, a living stone, rejected indeed of men, but with God elect, precious, ye also, as living stones, are built up a spiritual house, to be a holy priesthood, to offer up spiritual sacrifices, acceptable to God through Jesus Christ. Because it is contained in scripture,

> *Behold, I lay in Zion a chief corner stone, elect, precious:*
> *And he that believeth on him shall not be put to shame.*

For you therefore which believe is the preciousness: but for such as disbelieve,

> *The stone which the builders rejected,*
> *The same was made the head of the corner;*

and,

> *A stone of stumbling, and a rock of offence;*

for they stumble at the word, being disobedient: whereunto also they were appointed. But ye are an elect race, a royal priesthood, a holy nation, a people for God's own possession, that ye may shew forth the excellencies of him who called you out of darkness into his marvellous light: which in time past were no people, but now are the people of God: which had not obtained mercy, but now have obtained mercy.

St. Peter   I

2

Beloved, I beseech you as sojourners and pilgrims, to abstain from fleshly lusts, which war against the soul; having your behaviour seemly among the Gentiles; that, wherein they speak against you as evil-doers, they may by your good works, which they behold, glorify God in the day of visitation. Be subject to every ordinance of man for the Lord's sake: whether it be to the king, as supreme; or unto governors, as sent by him for vengeance on evil-doers and for praise to them that do well. For so is the will of God, that by well-doing ye should put to silence the ignorance of foolish men: as free, and not using your freedom for a cloke of wickedness, but as bondservants of God. Honour all men. Love the brotherhood. Fear God. Honour the king. Servants, be in subjection to your masters with all fear; not only to the good and gentle, but also to the froward. For this is acceptable, if for conscience toward God a man endureth griefs, suffering wrongfully. For what glory is it, if, when ye sin, and are buffeted for it, ye shall take it patiently? but if, when ye do well, and suffer for it, ye shall take it patiently, this is acceptable with God. For hereunto were ye called: because Christ also suffered for you, leaving you an example, that ye should follow his steps: who did no sin, neither was guile found in his mouth: who, when he was reviled, reviled not again; when he suffered, threatened not; but committed himself to him that judgeth righteously: who his own self bare our sins in his body upon the tree, that we, having died unto sins, might live unto righteousness; by whose stripes ye were healed. For ye were going astray like sheep; but are now returned unto the Shepherd and Bishop of your souls. In like manner, ye wives, be in subjection to your own husbands; that, even if any obey not the word, they may without the word be gained by the behaviour of their wives; beholding your chaste behaviour coupled with fear. Whose adorning let it not be the outward adorning of plaiting the hair, and of wearing jewels of gold, or of putting on apparel; but let it be the hidden man of the heart, in the incorruptible apparel of a meek and quiet spirit, which is in the sight of God of great price. For after this manner aforetime the holy women also, who hoped in God, adorned themselves, being in subjection to their own husbands: as Sarah obeyed Abraham, calling him lord: whose children ye now are, if ye do well, and are not put in fear by any terror. Ye husbands, in like manner, dwell with your wives according to knowledge, giving honour unto the woman, as unto the weaker vessel, as being also joint-heirs of the grace of life; to the end that your prayers be not hindered.

Finally, be ye all likeminded, compassionate, loving as brethren, tenderhearted, humbleminded: not rendering evil for evil, or reviling for reviling; but contrariwise blessing; for hereunto were ye called, that ye should inherit a blessing. For,

He that would love life,
And see good days,
Let him refrain his tongue from evil,
And his lips that they speak no guile:
And let him turn away from evil, and do good;
Let him seek peace, and pursue it.
For the eyes of the Lord are upon the righteous,
And his ears unto their supplication:
But the face of the Lord is upon them that do evil.

And who is he that will harm you, if ye be zealous of that which is good? But and if ye should suffer for righteousness' sake, blessed are ye: and fear not their fear, neither be troubled; but sanctify in your hearts Christ as Lord: being ready always to give answer to every man that asketh you a reason concerning the hope that is in you, yet with meekness and fear: having a good conscience; that, wherein ye are spoken against, they may be put to shame who revile your good manner of life in Christ. For it is better, if the will of God should so will, that ye suffer for well-doing than for evil-doing. Because Christ also suffered for sins once, the righteous for the unrighteous, that he might bring us to God; being put to death in the flesh — but quickened in the spirit: in which also he went and preached unto the spirits in prison, which aforetime were disobedient, when the longsuffering of God waited in the days of Noah, while the ark was a preparing, wherein few, that is, eight souls, were saved through water: (which also after a true likeness doth now save you, even baptism, not the putting away of the filth of the flesh, but the interrogation of a good conscience toward God, through the resurrection of Jesus Christ; who is on the right hand of God, having gone into heaven; angels and authorities and powers being made subject unto him:) — forasmuch then as Christ suffered in the flesh, arm ye yourselves also with the same mind (for he that hath suffered in the flesh hath ceased from sin) that ye no longer should live the rest of your time in the flesh to the lusts of men, but to the will of God. For the time past may suffice to have wrought the desire of the Gentiles, and to have walked in lasciviousness, lusts, winebibbings, revellings, carousings, and abominable idolatries: wherein they think it strange that ye run not with them into the same excess of riot, speaking evil of you: who shall give account to him that is ready to judge the quick and the dead. For unto this end was the gospel preached even to the dead, that they might be judged according to men in the flesh, but live according to God in the spirit.

3

But the end of all things is at hand: be ye therefore of sound mind, and be sober unto prayer: above all things being fervent in your love among yourselves; for love covereth a multitude of sins: using hospitality one to another without murmuring: according as each hath received a gift, ministering it among yourselves, as good stewards of the manifold grace of God; if any man speaketh, speaking as it were oracles of God; if any man ministereth, ministering as of the strength which God supplieth: that in all things God may be glorified through Jesus Christ, whose is the glory and the dominion for ever and ever. Amen. Beloved, think it not strange concerning the fiery trial among you, which cometh upon you to prove you, as though a strange thing happened unto you: but insomuch as ye are partakers of Christ's sufferings, rejoice; that at the revelation of his glory also ye may rejoice with exceeding joy. If ye are reproached for the name of Christ, blessed are ye; because the Spirit of glory and the Spirit of God resteth upon you. For let none of you suffer as a murderer, or a thief, or an evil-doer, or as a meddler in other men's matters: but if a man suffer as a Christian, let him not be ashamed; but let him glorify God in this name. For the time is come for judgement to begin at the house of God: and if it begin first at us, what shall be the end of them that obey not the gospel of God? And if the righteous is scarcely saved, where shall the ungodly and sinner appear? Wherefore let them also that suffer according to the will of God commit their souls in well-doing unto a faithful Creator. The elders therefore among you I exhort, who am a fellow-elder, and a witness of the sufferings of Christ, who am also a partaker of the glory that shall be revealed: Tend the flock of God which is among you, exercising the oversight, not of constraint, but willingly, according unto God; nor yet for filthy lucre, but of a ready mind; neither as lording it over the charge allotted to you, but making yourselves ensamples to the flock. And when the chief Shepherd shall be manifested, ye shall receive the crown of glory that fadeth not away. Likewise, ye younger, be subject unto the elder. Yea, all of you gird yourselves with humility, to serve one another: for God resisteth the proud, but giveth grace to the humble. Humble yourselves therefore under the mighty hand of God, that he may exalt you in due time; casting all your anxiety upon him, because he careth for you. Be sober, be watchful: your adversary the devil, as a roaring lion, walketh about, seeking whom he may devour: whom withstand stedfast in your faith, knowing that the same sufferings are accomplished in your brethren who are in the world. And the God of all grace, who called you unto his eternal glory in Christ, after that ye have suffered a little while, shall himself perfect, stablish, strengthen you. To him be the dominion for ever and ever. Amen.

By Silvanus, our faithful brother, as I account him, I have written unto you briefly, exhorting, and testifying

St. Peter

that this is the true grace of God: stand ye fast therein. She that is in Babylon, elect together with you, saluteth you: and so doth Mark my son. Salute one another with a kiss of love. Peace be unto you all that are in Christ.

The Epistles General

of

St. Peter

No. II

Simon Peter
A Servant and Apostle
of Jesus Christ

To them that have obtained a like precious faith with us in the righteousness of our God and Saviour Jesus Christ:

Grace to you and peace be multiplied in the knowledge of God and of Jesus our Lord; seeing that his divine power hath granted unto us all things that pertain unto life and godliness, through the knowledge of him that called us by his own glory and virtue; whereby he hath granted unto us his precious and exceeding great promises; that through these ye may become partakers of the divine nature, having escaped from the corruption that is in the world by lust. Yea, and for this very cause adding on your part all diligence, in your faith supply virtue; and in your virtue knowledge; and in your knowledge temperance; and in your temperance patience; and in your patience godliness; and in your godliness love of the brethren; and in your love of the brethren love. For if these things are yours and abound, they make you to be not idle nor unfruitful.

unto the knowledge of our Lord Jesus Christ. For he that lacketh these things is blind, seeing only what is near, having forgotten the cleansing from his old sins. Wherefore, brethren, give the more diligence to make your calling and election sure: for if ye do these things, ye shall never stumble: for thus shall be richly supplied unto you the entrance into the eternal kingdom of our Lord and Saviour Jesus Christ.

Wherefore I shall be ready always to put you in remembrance of these things, though ye know them, and are established in the truth which is with you. And I think it right, as long as I am in this tabernacle, to stir you up by putting you in remembrance; knowing that the putting off of my tabernacle cometh swiftly, even as our Lord Jesus Christ signified unto me. Yea, I will give diligence that at every time ye may be able after my decease to call these things to remembrance. For we did not follow cunningly devised fables, when we made known unto you the power and coming of our Lord Jesus Christ, but we were eyewitnesses of his majesty. For he received from God the Father honour and glory, when there came such a voice to him from the excellent glory, This is my beloved Son, in whom I am well pleased: and this voice we ourselves heard come out of heaven, when we were with him in the holy mount. And we have the word of prophecy made more sure; whereunto ye do well that ye take heed, as unto a lamp shining in a dark place, until the day dawn, and the day-star arise in your hearts: knowing this first, that no prophecy of scripture is of private interpretation; for no prophecy ever came by the will of man, but men spake from God, being moved by the Holy Ghost. But there arose false prophets also among the people, as among you also there shall be false teachers, who shall privily bring in destructive heresies, denying even the Master that bought them, bringing upon themselves swift destruction. And many shall follow their lascivious doings, by reason of whom the way of the truth shall be evil spoken of; and in covetousness shall they with feigned words make merchandise of you. Whose sentence now from of old lingereth not, and their destruction slumbereth not. For if God spared not angels when they sinned, but cast them down to hell, and committed them to pits of darkness, to be reserved unto judgement; and spared not the ancient world, but preserved Noah with seven others, a preacher of righteousness, when he brought a flood upon the world of the ungodly; and turning the cities of Sodom and Gomorrah into ashes condemned them with an overthrow, having made them an example unto those that should live ungodly; and delivered righteous Lot, sore distressed by the lascivious life of the wicked (for that righteous man dwelling among them, in seeing and hearing, vexed his righteous soul from day to day with their lawless deeds): the Lord knoweth how to deliver the godly out of temptation, and to keep the unrighteous under punishment unto the day of judgement; but chiefly them that walk after the flesh in the lust of defilement, and despise dominion. Daring, selfwilled, they tremble not to rail at dignities: whereas angels, though greater in might and power, bring not a railing judgement against them before the Lord. But these, as creatures without reason, born mere animals to be taken and destroyed, railing in matters whereof they are ignorant, shall in their destroying surely be destroyed, suffering wrong as the hire of wrongdoing; men that count it pleasure to revel in the day-time, spots and blemishes, revelling in their love-feasts while they feast with you; having eyes full of adultery, and that cannot cease from sin; enticing unstedfast souls; having a heart exercised in covetousness; children of cursing; forsaking the right way, they went astray, having followed the way of Balaam the son of Beor, who loved the hire of wrong-doing, but he was rebuked for his own transgression—a dumb ass spake with man's voice and stayed the madness of the prophet. These are springs without water, and mists driven by a storm; for whom the blackness of darkness hath been reserved. For, uttering great swelling words of vanity, they entice in the lusts of the flesh, by lasciviousness, those who are just escaping from them that live in error; promising them liberty, while they themselves are bondservants of corruption: for of whom a man is overcome, of the same is he also brought into bondage. For if, after they have escaped the defilements of the world through the knowledge of the Lord and Saviour Jesus Christ, they are again entangled therein and overcome, the last state is become worse with them than the first. For it were better for them not to have known the way of righteousness, than, after knowing it, to turn back from the holy commandment delivered unto them. It has happened unto them according to the true proverb, The dog turning to his own vomit again, and the sow that had washed to wallowing in the mire.

This is now, beloved, the second epistle that I write unto you; and in both of them I stir up your sincere mind by putting you in remembrance; that ye should remember the words which were spoken before by the holy prophets, and the commandment of the Lord and Saviour through your apostles: knowing this first, that in the last days mockers shall come with mockery, walking after their own lusts, and saying, Where is the promise of his coming? for, from the day that the fathers fell asleep, all things continue as they were from the beginning of the creation. For this they wilfully forget, that there were heavens from of old, and an earth compacted out of water and amidst water, by the word of God; by which means the world that then was, being overflowed with water, perished: but the heavens that now are, and the earth, by the same word have been stored up for fire, being reserved against the day of judgement and destruction of ungodly men.

But forget not this one thing, beloved, that one day is with the Lord as a thousand years, and a thousand years as one day. The Lord is not slack concerning his promise, as some count slackness; but is longsuffering to you-ward, not wishing that any should perish, but that all should come to repentance. But the day of the Lord will come as a thief; in the which the heavens shall pass away with a great noise, and the elements shall be dissolved with fervent heat, and the earth and the works that are therein shall be burned up. Seeing that these things are thus all to be dissolved, what manner of persons ought ye to be in all holy living and godliness, looking for and earnestly desiring the coming of the day of God, by reason of which the heavens being on fire shall be dissolved, and the elements shall melt with fervent heat? But, according to his promise, we look for new heavens and a new earth, wherein dwelleth righteousness. Wherefore, beloved, seeing that ye look for these things, give diligence that ye may be found in peace, without spot and blameless in his sight. And account that the long-suffering of our Lord is salvation; even as our beloved brother Paul also, according to the wisdom given to him, wrote unto you; as also in all his epistles, speaking in them of these things; wherein are some things hard to be understood, which the ignorant and unstedfast wrest, as they do also the other scriptures, unto their own destruction. Ye therefore, beloved, knowing these things beforehand, beware lest, being carried away with the error of the wicked, ye fall from your own stedfastness. But grow in the grace and knowledge of our Lord and Saviour Jesus Christ. To him be the glory both now and for ever. Amen.

AN EPISTLE GENERAL

OF

ST. JUDE

Judas
*A Servant of Jesus
Christ and Brother
of James*

To them that are called, beloved in God the Father, and kept for Jesus Christ:

*Mercy unto you
and Peace and Love
be multiplied.*

BELOVED, while I was giving all diligence to write unto you of our common salvation, I was constrained to write unto you exhorting you to contend earnestly for the faith which was once for all delivered unto the saints. For there are certain men crept in privily, even they who were of old set forth unto this condemnation, ungodly men, turning the grace of our God into lasciviousness, and denying our only Master and Lord, Jesus Christ.

Now I desire to put you in remembrance, though ye know all things once for all, how that the Lord, having saved a people out of the land of Egypt, afterward destroyed them that believed not. And angels which kept not their own principality, but left their proper habitation, he hath kept in everlasting bonds under darkness unto the judgement of the great day. Even as Sodom and Gomorrah, and the cities about them, having in like manner with these given themselves over to fornication, and gone after strange flesh, are set forth as an example, suffering the punishment of eternal fire. Yet in like manner these also in their dreamings defile the flesh, and set at nought dominion, and rail at dignities. But Michael the archangel, when contending with the devil he disputed about the body of Moses, durst not bring against him a railing judgement, but said, The Lord rebuke thee. But these rail at whatsoever things they know not: and what they understand naturally, like the creatures without reason, in these things are they destroyed. Woe unto them! for they went in the way of Cain, and ran riotously in the error of Balaam for hire, and perished in the gainsaying of Korah. These are they who are hidden rocks in your love-feasts when they feast with you, shepherds that without fear feed themselves; clouds without water, carried along by winds; autumn trees without fruit, twice dead, plucked up by the roots; wild waves of the sea, foaming out their own shame; wandering stars, for whom the blackness of darkness hath been reserved for ever. And to these also Enoch, the seventh from Adam, prophesied, saying, Behold, the Lord came with ten thousands of his holy ones, to execute judgement upon all, and to

St. Jude

convict all the ungodly of all their works of ungodliness which they have ungodly wrought, and of all the hard things which ungodly sinners have spoken against him. These are murmurers, complainers, walking after their lusts (and their mouth speaketh great swelling words), shewing respect of persons for the sake of advantage. But ye, beloved, remember ye the words which have been spoken before by the apostles of our Lord Jesus Christ; how that they said to you, In the last time there shall be mockers, walking after their own ungodly lusts. These are they who make separations, sensual, having not the Spirit. But ye, beloved, building up yourselves on your most holy faith, praying in the Holy Spirit, keep yourselves in the love of God, looking for the mercy of our Lord Jesus Christ unto eternal life. And on some have mercy, who are in doubt; and some save, snatching them out of the fire; and on some have mercy with fear; hating even the garment spotted by the flesh.

Now unto him that is able to guard you from stumbling, and to set you before the presence of his glory without blemish in exceeding joy, to the only God our Saviour, through Jesus Christ our Lord, be glory, majesty, dominion and power, before all time, and now, and for evermore. Amen.

NOTES TO THE GOSPELS

ST. MATTHEW

The Genealogy

There is in this genealogy a superficial discrepancy in the fact that the details do not seem to bear out the *fourteen generations* claimed for each of the three divisions. This, however, can be explained without the assumption (sometimes made) that David and Jechoniah are counted twice over. (1) Abraham and Jesus, the starting-point and the conclusion, are both counted in: this is the 'inclusive manner of reckoning,' by which the Hebrews would call the period from Friday afternoon to Sunday morning three days. This at once brings the first division to the requisite number fourteen, and the third division to thirteen. (2) It is obvious that *generation* in the strict sense can be carried no further than Joseph. Between him and Jesus the mother Mary is interposed: when she is reckoned as one the number fourteen is completed.

I, II

Page 9. *Behold the virgin shall be with child*, etc. — page 11. *Out of Egypt did I call my son.* — page 16. *The land of Zebulun*, etc.: compare *Isaiah*, chapter vii. 14 and ix. 1; *Hosea*, xi. 1. New Testament writers, and especially Matthew, seem often to cite sentences of the O.T. apart from their historical context, as seeing a mystic significance in the very phrases of Scripture. For the first citation, and the name *Immanuel*, compare the *Isaiah* volume of this series, pages 223-30; for the third, pages 31 and 229.

III — St. Matthew

Page 12. *He shall be called a Nazarene:* the reference has not been identified. Some suppose *Nazarene* to be a term of reproach (compare, "Out of Galilee ariseth no prophet"), and that the reference is to such a passage as *Isaiah*, chapter liii. 1, 2.

III

After a few sentences describing the opening of Christ's ministry, this section is wholly occupied with the collection of sayings which has come to be known as 'The Sermon on the Mount.' The general suggestion is that it is a collection from several discourses, many of them delivered very likely from a hill slope, as a favourite mode of public speaking, and drawn together into their present arrangement by the evangelist as a full type of the teaching of Jesus in the early part of his ministry. The sayings are sayings of Jesus; the arrangement is that of St. Matthew. This explains the occurrence in St. Luke's gospel of a collection of sayings having so much in common with the present collection as to suggest identity; yet much briefer, different in form, and associated with different surroundings. Both writers are giving specimens or resumés of the general teaching that characterised an epoch in Christ's life.

The arrangement adopted by St. Matthew is that of a literary form very common in Wisdom literature. It may be called the 'Maxim' [*Ecclesiasticus* volume, page xi]: and consists of a gnomic sentence by way of text, followed by a prose comment or expansion. These 'maxims' form a characteristic part of *Ecclesiasticus* and *Ecclesiastes*, with the former of which Jesus shows familiarity [*Ecclesiasticus* volume, page xxxii]: it continues a form of writing to the time of the *Epistle of St. James* [above, page 201]. But that the word has lost its proper significance to modern ears, the discourse might be appropriately entitled, 'The Wisdom of Jesus.' The whole discourse in St. Matthew's arrangement falls into seven sections: six are expansions each of a single gnomic saying, expressive of some fundamental conception of the new kingdom. The seventh section is miscellaneous: strings of disconnected sayings following more connected argument are a highly characteristic feature of Wisdom literature [compare the *Ecclesiastes* volume, page 35]. The number of sayings in this seventh section are seven, and the opening section has a sevenfold expansion of its text: this domination of Matthew's writings by the number seven has been noted in the Introduction.

1. In accordance with the general scheme of the whole discourse, this first section must be read, not as a string of eight beatitudes, but as a single beatitude with a sevenfold expansion. The beatitude brings forward a leading conception of Christ's new kingdom: the way in which it is to reverse accepted ideas of what is greatness. Thus the significance of the term *poor in spirit* must be looked for in the seven applications into which it is expanded:

> mourning — in contrast with gaiety: compare such passages as *Ecclesiastes*, chapter vii. 2.
> *the meek* — in contrast with the territorial magnate: just the contrast emphasised in *Job*, chapter xxii. 6-9.

they that hunger and thirst after righteousness: the sense of higher spiritual attainments to be sought — in contrast with Pharisaic satisfaction with external righteousness: the contrast of the publican and the Pharisee.

the merciful — in contrast with the oppressive.

the pure in heart — in contrast with the worldly: the thought of *Psalms* xxiv and xv. As these psalms describe such purity as preparation for God's house, the conclusion here is natural, *they shall see God.*

the peacemaker — in contrast with the warrior.

finally, with full details bearing upon those addressed: the persecuted — in contrast with his persecutor.

ii. The significance is clear: Salt is not food, but that which is used to keep food wholesome; if the church is ceasing to influence the world its very *raison d'être* is gone.

iii. *Ye are the light of the world.* Of this gnomic saying a twofold application is made: (1) As you are the world's spiritual leaders, no action of yours can escape observation. — (2) It is the function of light to shine: unless you make goodness attractive to outsiders you are failing in your mission.

iv. The new kingdom is not a relaxation of the law, but a carrying of it on to its perfection. — Agree *with thine adversary . . . thou shalt by no means come out,* etc. This whole passage is not a fresh command, but an illustration. The theme has been anger, and its rising stages of intensity. This is illustrated by the successive stages of legal process: subdue anger in the early stage, and so escape the bitter end.

Notes &   III v–vii

v. The text is the heavenly and not the earthward reference of all spiritual acts.—Page 23. *Our Father which art in heaven,* etc. The structure of this first part of the Lord's Prayer is important for the exact sense. As ordinarily printed the passage is made a series of separate petitions: *Hallowed be thy name. Thy kingdom come. Thy will be done as in heaven so on earth.* By this arrangement the words *as in heaven,* etc., are made to apply only to the last petition, *Thy will be done.* I have printed the whole as an 'envelope figure,' which connects the beginning and the end with all that comes between; thus the full sense implied is, *Hallowed be thy name, as in heaven, so on earth — Thy kingdom come, as in heaven, so on earth — Thy will be done, as in heaven, so on earth.*

vi. *The lamp of the body is the eye.* That which we 'have an eye to' is what gives the light of purpose to all our actions; if the very light-making part of us be darkness, what must be the gloom of the rest of us (the darkness).

vii. As remarked above, this section is made up of seven miscellaneous sayings. — 2. In this saying again parallelism of structure is an important light upon exact meaning. As printed in the text it will be observed that the first and fourth lines have common indentation, and again the second and third: thus the sense is:

Give *not that which is holy unto the dogs,*
    Neither *cast your pearls before the swine:*
        Lest *haply they* [the swine] *trample them under their feet,*
And [the dogs] *turn and rend you.*

Throw a bone, if you want to propitiate a dog: if you throw him something sacred, he will smell at it a moment and then be at you. So, cast pearls to swine and they will trample them without deigning to notice. The application in both cases is to want of spiritual appreciation: spiritual things must be spiritually discerned.

IV.

In this, as in all sections, we have general incidents of teaching and healing: especially such works of power as are recorded in ii and iv. The distinctiveness of section IV is however clear. (1) It contains the First Impressions made by the ministry of Jesus: especially the teaching *with authority*, which made so startling a contrast to all that was then in vogue, — (2) With this we have the Gathering of Disciples: the incident of the scribe (i), in view of the future hostility of this class, suggests the eagerness with which the call was being responded to. — (3) There are also Hints of the Antagonism that was about to manifest itself: in i the words to the centurion suggest how the Gentiles were about to welcome what the children of the kingdom would reject; in ii a whole city is offended; iii is occupied with questionings as to forgiveness of sins, eating in company with outcasts, abstinence from fasting. The section reaches an appropriate conclusion in an incident which rouses the multitude to enthusiasm, and calls from Pharisees mutterings of the thought which was hereafter to be their great blasphemy.

i. *See thou tell no man; but . . . shew thyself to the priest*, etc. The latter part of the command illustrates the care with which Jesus avoids a conflict with the existing ecclesiastical

Notes on IV

system, so far as this is innocent: compare (X. iv) *The scribes and the Pharisees sit on Moses' seat : all things therefore whatsoever they bid you, these do and observe.* It is part of his fixed purpose to extend his kingdom to the Gentiles through the chosen people, if they will accept the duty; and this explains the words to the Canaanite woman (VIII. iv), and the charge to the Apostles (V. 1), as well as the Ascension charge which is the basis of the *Acts of the Apostles*. The former part of the command [compare below (iv), *sternly charged them*] reflects the fixed purpose of Jesus to avoid unsettling men's minds by appeals to wonder and excitement, which leads Matthew (VI. iii) to apply to him the Isaiahan prophecy, *He shall not strive nor cry*. His appeal is to spiritual evidence: hence [*Mark* ii, vi] he checks the acknowledgments from demons, and [*Matthew* VI. iv] indignantly refuses the demand for a sign from heaven. When [as recorded by *St. John*, chapter xiv. 11] he says to the doubting disciples, *Or else believe me for the very works' sake*, he is descending to meet the adversaries on their own ground. — In the same spirit he commands [IX. i] the disciples to tell no man the wonder of the transfiguration until the time of his resurrection: he will not have the revelation of his glory stand apart from the revelation of his sufferings.

Page 31. *The foxes have holes*, etc. . . . *leave the dead to bury their own dead.* The purport of both incidents seems to be the same: the eagerness at this period in responding to the new call needs to be so far checked as that aspirants are bidden to count the cost.

V ◦⊕ St. Matthew

V

The Commission to the Apostles, which is the subject of this section, is an excellent illustration of the principle underlying the whole of St. Matthew's writing, how he gathers from various parts of Christ's life sayings which he masses together at the point where they will be most effective. The Commission in the other gospels is brief. But Mark [chapters iii. 14 and vi. 7] seems to speak of more than one expedition of the twelve; Luke records this and also a similar expedition of seventy: the suggestion is that Christ sent out many such expeditions. Significant portions of the charge appear in the other gospels in connection with the expeditions: Matthew once for all gives a full and elaborate commission. It has the sevenfold division which is his strong characteristic:

1. Limitation to Israel.
2. The two works of preaching and healing.
3. It is not a hired ministry.
4. On the other hand, it is not to be at the cost of the missionary: simple hospitality is to be accepted.
5. Attitude to the inevitable opposition.
6. Great doctrine of the kingdom: outwardly a kingdom of peace it brings spiritual warfare into every household.
7. For those accepting the word reward is certain, but it is spiritual [*a prophet's reward*].

Page 38. *For there is nothing covered that shall not be revealed*, etc. The general connection makes these words, not a promise

Notes VI

to the apostles, but a restatement of their duty. They are fearlessly to exercise their function of being the light of the world; for the special privileges [compare the whole of VII and its indication of an inner circle and doctrine] which have been accorded them have been given on the express condition that they shall impart to others what has been spoken to them in the privacy of the circle of disciples. That this is the connection of thought is clear from the fact that in *Mark* (chapter iv. 22) the words *There is nothing covered*, etc. directly follow the image of the lamp or candle, significant of the function of the disciples to make their doctrine known. [Compare *Luke*, chapter xii. 2–3.] This cannot be affected by the fact that in *Luke* (chapter xii. 2) the proverbial saying, *There is nothing covered*, etc., is put in antithesis to the hypocrisy of the Pharisees.

VI

I have entitled this section 'The Growing Isolation of Jesus and his Ministry.' Successive sections bring out (i) his reluctant separation from the ministry of John, greatest of ministers, yet still outside the kingdom of heaven — (ii) his separation from the might and wisdom of the cities: he thankfully turns to the meek and lowly — (iii) his separation from the Pharisaic doctrine of the Sabbath, most distinctive of Jewish institutions — (iv) open antagonism to the now open blasphemy of the Pharisees, and the appeal of other scribes and Pharisees for physical and not spiritual wonders. — As a climax to this section, Matthew records here a sense of separation even from mother and brethren in response to the call of his divine mission.

i. *Art thou he that cometh*, etc. The suggestion is an impatience on the part of John the Baptist for some grand assertion of Messiahship; the reports of Jesus were not *the works of the Christ* which he was expecting. The answer of Jesus is, as always, an appeal to spiritual evidence: healing and good tidings, not wonders. The final words bid John not make an offence of this confinement of miracle to works of mercy.

In the discourse that follows Jesus does enthusiastic justice to the grandeur of John, yet recognises his ministry as below the kingdom of heaven.—*The kingdom of heaven suffereth violence ... all the prophets and the law prophesied until John:* the period of passive acquiescence in a law and external righteousness gives place, with John, to a period when righteousness must be active, nay, a violent pressing in to the kingdom. This is the general spirit of III. iv.

Page 42. *It is like unto children. . . . But wisdom is justified by her children.* The image is of children's games: they cannot agree among themselves whether to play funeral or wedding, and the sport is spoiled. Meanwhile, both in John's ministry and Christ's, those who are children of Wisdom recognise the truth [compare the use of *justified* in *Luke* (chapter vii. 29): *the people ... justified God*, gave their verdict on his side, in contrast with the Pharisees and lawyers, who *rejected the counsel of God*].

ii. *All things have been delivered unto me of my Father.* The connection of thought seems to be this: he has just recognised

Notes & VI iv

his rejection by the great; by the authority committed to him from the Father he solemnly turns from the strong· to the humble: *Come unto me, all ye that labour*, etc.

iv. The internal connection of this important section, though not obvious, must be insisted upon. (1) The incident of the mother and brethren is linked to that of the Pharisaic blasphemy in *Mark* (section vii), and even in *Matthew* the phrase, *While he was yet speaking*, etc., is a link. (2) In *Luke* (chapter xi) the whole discussion of the 'sign' is closely bound up with the incident of the blasphemy. (3) In the present case the latter part of Christ's answer to the demand for a sign (see below) seems to sum up by parable the position of both objectors.

The incident is opened by the bold words of some Pharisees, ascribing to demonic agency Christ's casting out of demons. After calmly exposing the self-contradiction of the suggestion, Jesus, with gathering indignation, goes on to denounce this as worse than antagonism to himself, being nothing less than blasphemy against the Divine Spirit of Healing, which is to Jesus the highest spiritual evidence. — *It shall not be forgiven him, neither in this world, nor in that which is to come:* these words are not a threat, but picture the hopeless state of such blasphemers [compare (*Mark*, section vii): *is guilty of an eternal sin*]; antagonism to the spirit of healing is manifestly unhealable. — *Either make the tree good*, etc. . . . *every idle word that men shall speak*, etc.: the argument continues: such blasphemy implies an inward unsoundness deeper than their words [possibly *idle words* suggests a violent thing said in the heat of controversy]; though even their words will be an element in the judgment. Another body of the opponents interrupt, clamouring for a 'sign' [*Luke* in a similar passage on the same incident has *a sign from heaven, i.e.* beyond the power of magic]. Originally, the 'sign of the prophet' was the symbol or emblem which constituted the text of his discourse, such as the soiled girdle of Jeremiah, or the potter's bottle which he broke in token of the coming doom of the chosen people. But as some of these signs came miraculously (*e.g.* in Amos's visions), there grew in time a greater interest in the miraculous sign than in the spiritual truth of which it was the vehicle. Such decadence in the attitude to prophecy is precisely what Jesus sets himself steadily to oppose — the mere wonder at miraculous power taking the place of recognition of the spiritual grace of healing; he sets himself to suppress the natural fame of his healing wonders. Accordingly the demand at this point for a 'sign' is a less pronounced form of the previous blasphemy; it is a rejection of the supreme spiritual evidence implied in healing powers, and a preference for the vulgar exercise of mere physical power. It is treated accordingly as an evidence of spiritual degeneration [*an evil and adulterous generation*]: and for a 'sign' Jesus goes back to the true meaning of the term and offers the 'sign of Jonah': the great symbol of preaching and repentance. To this is added the Queen of Sheba, great symbol of sitting at the feet of Wisdom. Addressing both bodies of objectors at once, Jesus then speaks the parable which has application to the evil at the root of both — the rejection of the supreme spirit of healing: the inherently unclean spirit, returning to his cleansed home, makes it the home of yet greater uncleanness.

Notes

Page 47: footnote. Here, as elsewhere in this series of books, I have made use of the modern device of footnotes to separate sentences which, from the absence of such devices in ancient manuscripts, sometimes make awkward parentheses and interrupt the drift of thought. I understand the words, *For as Jonah was three days and three nights in the belly of the whale*, etc., to be a reflection of St. Matthew, and not part of the discourse of Jesus. (1) The 'sign of Jonah' occurs three times [*Matthew*, chapter xvi. 4; *Luke*, chapter xi. 29–33]: only in this passage is there any reference to the incident of the whale. In all three passages the natural meaning of the 'sign of Jonah' is that he is a sign of *repentance* to the Ninevites: this is put positively, and twice over, in the passage of *Luke;* while the strongly rhetorical cast, both of the present passage and that in *Luke*, makes the intrusion of a different image most unlikely.— (2) Again, a reference to the death and resurrection of Christ at this point is entirely out of keeping with the fixed order of narrative in the synoptic gospels, according to which no suggestion of the death of the Master appears until the complete recognition of him in his Messiahship by Peter and the disciples, from which point it dominates the whole narrative [compare above (page 64): *From that time began Jesus to shew unto his disciples*, etc.]. References recorded by St. John in incidents usually understood to be earlier cannot affect the question: they belong to Judæa and individual conversations; this reference to the period of Christ's lying in the tomb would be unintelligible to the persons here addressed.— (3) On the other hand, the words contain precisely the kind of reflection on

VII   St. Matthew

minute fulfilment of prophecy which is a leading characteristic of St. Matthew; and the utterance, pointless in the speech of Jesus, is a natural reflection for one who writes after the resurrection. — (4) No difficulty arises from the tense, *so shall the Son of man be:* the writer naturally puts himself at the point of view of the incident that raises his reflection. There is a very similar case in connection with the dream of Joseph (page 9): after the words of the angel " Thou shalt call his name ' Jesus,' " etc., we read, " Now all this is come to pass that it might be fulfilled which was spoken," etc., — as if this recognition of prophecy was part of the dream. Yet I presume no one would so interpret it: not a trace of it is found in the announcement of the angel to Mary, as recorded in *Luke.*

VII

All three evangelists treat the matter of this section in such a way as to suggest that it makes an epoch in the ministry of Jesus. Parables of course occur at other points: but here the Public Parable and the Private Interpretation becomes for a time a distinctive mode of teaching, suggestive of an outer and inner doctrine for the new dispensation. The suggestion is further assisted by the phrase, *Unto you it is given to know the mysteries of the kingdom of heaven:* ' mysteries ' is a technical term of ancient religions, implying the two elements of mystic symbols for the outside world, and the full understanding of them only for ' the initiated.' To the same effect is the suggestion of the concluding words: that the inner circle of disciples are the 'scribes' of the new dispensation. We have seen above (note to page 38) the warning that such special privileges are granted them only that they may be used for the public hereafter.   The arrangement of the section is clear. According to his usual practice, Matthew represents the general parabolic teaching of Jesus by *seven* parables. There is an interruption after the first, and the whole plan of public parable and private interpretation is explained, while the foundation parable of the Sower is interpreted. Later on there is another interruption, as if further to illustrate the plan of teaching: for it will be observed that the parable then interpreted is not the one last delivered. At the end there is a formal conclusion, as if by a completed course of training the disciples are recognised as fully instructed 'scribes.'

Page 54. *A man that is a householder ... things new and old.* The words merely imply that they are well furnished for their teaching. Possibly the latter phrase suggests ever new interpretations of old sayings.

VIII

This section is occupied with (1) the Greater Miracles. They are greater in the sense of being more impressive and wide-reaching in their effects. The feeding of multitudes directly associates itself with the pressure of crowds upon the ministry of Jesus, which is a link of connection throughout this part of the narrative; and to the wider fame may be due the deputation from Jerusalem (iii). Again, the miracle on the

VIII ii, iii ⇥ St. Matthew

sea draws from the disciples who alone witness it the anticipation of that full recognition which is the basis of section IX.— (2) *The Growing Antagonism*. In i his own country takes offence at Jesus; in iii the deputation from Jerusalem leads to his open renunciation of the Tradition of the Elders, which was the distinctive religion of the age.

ii. The starting-point is the announcement of John's execution. From the tender affection he cherishes for his precursor Jesus feels this as a personal bereavement, and seeks retirement: the multitudes press upon his privacy and follow him to the desert, which leads to the miracle of feeding; seeking retirement in the night he is separated from the disciples, and his rejoining them brings the miracle on the sea; upon the arrival at the land there is fresh crowding, and so we reach iii and the deputation from Jerusalem.

iii. The Tradition of the Elders was the organised form finally taken by the long-continued idolatry of the very letter of the Mosaic Law. It was not enough to abstain from actual breaches of this Law: a 'hedge about the Law' had been made, in the form of traditional practices designed to avoid even doubtful acts. In process of time these minute traditions had, in the thoughts of the religious world, taken the place of the Law itself. Jesus is for ever appealing from the outward letter to the inner spirit: and in the present incident openly pronounces against the whole traditional system. How great a shock this was to the religious spirit of the time is measured by the difficulty with which even the disciples receive the appeal to inner as against outer purity.

Notes

iv. Jesus, still in search of quiet, retires to the region of Canaanite cities outside the range he has prescribed for his personal ministry [compare above, note to IV. i]. He allows himself to be spiritually forced by the faith of the Canaanite woman.

v. On his return, Jesus, still in search of quiet, is in the desert parts of Galilee, and is again oppressed by the widespread influence of the miracle of feeding; again he exercises his ministry, and a second time works a miracle of feeding. This leads to a fresh deputation of rulers, and another demand for a 'sign,' which is answered as before (above, note to VI. iv). The miracle and the discussion are both involved in the subsequent discourse on 'leaven.'

IX

The turning-point in Matthew's narrative of the Ministry of Jesus is made by the Confession of Peter, and full recognition of the Messiahship by the band of disciples, followed immediately by the visible glory of the Transfiguration. This leads to the revelation by Jesus of his sufferings and death, reserved till after this recognition: the union of the two ideas of kingship and suffering makes the whole 'mystery' of the kingdom into which the disciples are to be initiated. Their intense difficulty in understanding the union of these ideas leads to a series of Questions concerning the kingdom, and with these the whole section is occupied. Its natural divisions are divisions of locality.— i. The Confession takes place in *the parts of Cæsarea Philippi:* in this neighbourhood arises the first of the questionings, as to the coming of Elijah.—ii. In Galilee there is fresh inculcation of the doctrine of the suffering Messiah. An external circumstance (the demand for toll) brings up the whole question, wherein consists greatness in the kingdom of heaven; and out of the discussion of this arises a kindred question of sin and its treatment under the new dispensation.— iii. The scene has changed to *the borders of Judæa beyond Jordan*. Here two external incidents give rise to two discussions: questions of marriage, and again of mammon, are raised in relation to the kingdom of heaven.— iv. In *the going up to Jerusalem* the nearer expectation of the kingdom leads, through a demand of the sons of Zebedee, to a new aspect of Christ's kingdom: lordship in it is service.

i. *Thou art 'Peter,' and upon this 'rock,'* etc.: in the original the two words have a resemblance of sense and sound: *Petros* and *Petra*.

ii. The link binding together the parts of this subsection is found in the idea of 'offence': *lest we cause them to stumble, go thou to the sea*, etc. Payment of toll seems incongruous with the newly recognised kingship: Jesus admits it, yet pays, to avoid offence. This not unnaturally raises the question of greatness in this novel kingdom [compare, "Who *then* is greatest," etc.]. Christ's answer is the object-lesson of the child, and the care to avoid giving offence even to the least: to avoid giving offence to these his disciples must forego what is most positively their own—the hand, the foot, the eye—caring more even for the stray sheep than the ninety-nine at home. The transition is to offences against one's self, and actual sins: these are to be

Notes   IX ii, iii

encountered, not by power, but by the reference to the spirit of the new society [*tell it unto the church*]; if even this fails, there is no more of violence than that the offender is to be held as outside the society [*let him be unto thee as the Gentile and the publican*]. The connection of the words that follow [*What things soever ye shall bind on earth*, etc.] is that this society and its relations to its members is pronounced the only power for dealing with offences that Christ will recognise in his kingdom. — A further question of Peter, as to how far this treatment is to be carried, leads to the declaration that it is unlimited: this is emphasised by the parable which brings out that all differences of offences as between man and man vanish in the vast gulf between sinful man and the forgiving God.

Page 69. *I say not unto thee, Until seven times; but, Until Seventy times and seven.* I have preferred the marginal reading of the R.V. here, because it preserves the echo of Lamech's *Song of the Sword* [*Genesis* volume, page 14]:

If Cain shall be avenged sevenfold,
Truly Lamech seventy and sevenfold.

The law of Christian forgiveness is made commensurate with the traditional song of revenge.

iii. The question raised of Divorce comes from the outside; its importance for the spirit of this part of the narrative consists in the further question raised by Christ's ruling in the mind of the disciples: If this be so, what is the good of marriage? The reply is, Even this may have to be given up for the kingdom's sake. — In the second discussion (on mammon) the connection of thought seems to be as follows. Mammon is opposed to the spirituality of the kingdom. When with difficulty this has been accepted the disciples ask, What then shall be our reward who are giving up everything? The answer is, Reward they shall have indeed, but not measured on any economic scale of graduation: the first may be last and the last first. This is enforced by the Parable of the Hired Labourers.

X

The order of narrative is clear and simple: the Royal Entry into Jerusalem, the successive conflicts with various classes of opponents, and the final breach with the rulers of the religious world. From this point Christ retires from public ministry, and the narrative follows his discourses to his disciples.

i. Incident of the Fig Tree. The suggestiveness of this incident must be gathered from the position in the narrative in which it is found. The fig tree catches the eye of Jesus as he is approaching Jerusalem in this period of his final breach with the holy city and the religious rebellion it represents. It must be remembered that the barren fig tree had already been the subject of a parable [*Luke*, chapter xiii. 6] by which, at a time when the antagonism of the Jews had not yet reached its crisis, Jesus expressed long patience and a time of respite: there should be yet a year for digging and manuring, if perchance even yet the barren might bear fruit. Now that Jesus is on his way to the final casting off of the guilty city his eye is caught by the tree with its fair show of leaves and no fruit; he is reminded of his own parable, and solemnly pronounces that the offered respite is at an end: *Let there be no fruit from thee henceforward for ever.* But this natural significance of the incident is veiled by the perversity of the disciples, who, sharing the universal tendency to fix on the physical miracle and not the spiritual truth, are struck by the marvel of the fig tree's actually withering away. Jesus takes the opportunity for enforcing a lesson of faith and its power to work wonders.

iv. Here St. Matthew, according to his custom, gathers into one carefully arranged discourse, the succession of sayings of Jesus in which he expresses his final denunciation of the scribes and Pharisees. Its structure shows (1) a general introduction, (2) a sevenfold woe, modelled by St. Matthew upon the Sevenfold Woe of Isaiah [page 16 of that volume], and (3) a conclusion expressing the yearning over the fate of the doomed city.

Page 87. "*Therefore, behold I send unto you,*" etc. The words in quotation marks I understand to be words of God, not of Jesus. In rhetorical vehemence he unifies the whole hostility of the Pharisaic spirit, past as well as present and future, in one continuous opposition to God's will.

XI

This discourse appears in all three gospels in closely similar sections, except that Matthew, according to his custom, expands it to a sevenfold division. [Compare above note to V.] The question of the disciples puts together *thy coming and the end of the world*, as if they constituted the same thing. It is a leading point of Christ's answer to separate the two, and this is a key to the sections of the discourse. — 1. He shows that every tribulation is not the end: they must beware of the cries of Christ's coming which these tribulations may give rise to. — 2. He then deals with the tribulation of Judæa: [this is so far the 'coming of Christ' that it is the fall of the power that has opposed him:] but the lightninglike coming of the Son of man in the true sense is different. — 3. After that tribulation will suddenly [note: *immediately, after:* not, *immediately after:* compare corresponding passages of *Mark* and *Luke*] be a greater tribulation: a shaking of the heavens, and the Son of man shall be seen coming in glory. — 4. The one tribulation can be told by signs, as are read the signs of coming spring in the fig tree: the other will come by surprise, and none but the Father knows when. — 5. The moral is watchfulness, and this is enforced by the Parable of the Ten Virgins. — 6. With watchfulness is combined work: Parable of the Talents. — 7. As a final section St. Matthew records the description of the last judgment.

XII

The narrative in this final section of *St. Matthew* is transparently simple and the divisions obvious: The preparations for the end — the Last Supper — the scenes on Olivet — the preliminary Examination before Caiaphas — the Trial before Pilate — the Crucifixion — the Burial — the Resurrection and Ascension.

i. The link binding together the three paragraphs of this

Notes

subsection is the circumstance, recorded by St. John, that the speaker of the words, *To what purpose is this waste*, etc., was Judas.

Page 98. *This is my blood of the covenant*, etc.: see below, note to page 188.

Page 103. *That which was spoken by Jeremiah the prophet:* the passage apparently referred to is found in our *Book of Zechariah*, chapter xi. 13. Similarly in *Mark* i a passage is cited as from 'Isaiah' of which the first portion is from our *Book of Malachi*, chapter iii. 1, the latter from our *Book of Isaiah*, chapter xl. 3. Just as the name 'David' stands for the psalms in general, and 'Solomon' for all wisdom literature, so the whole roll of prophecy may be cited by the names of the two most prominent prophets. There are traces of different rolls of the prophets commencing severally with Isaiah and Jeremiah. But the naturalness of this is increased if, as there is reason to suppose, the latter part of our *Zechariah*, and *Malachi*, were originally anonymous books of prophecy. See the Minor Prophets volume of this series, pages v-vii.

ST. MARK

As already stated in the Introduction the gospel of St. Mark takes the literary form of independent sections, narrating successive incidents, rather than that of a regularly arranged history.

Page 113. *As it is written in Isaiah the prophet:* see above, note to page 103.

ii. This section seems to be giving a general picture of the ministry of Jesus, with illustrative particulars. Most of it is a specimen day of work in Capernaum.

iii. A note of this section, and of a good deal of St. Mark's gospel, is the suggestion of the crowding upon Jesus, produced by the fame of his miracles.

Page 116. *See thou say nothing to any man:* see above, note to *Matthew* IV. i.

iv. The two incidents of this section are connected together by the three evangelists, but Mark preserves the link between them: that the feast in Matthew's house took place while John's disciples and the Pharisees were observing a fast.

vi. While this section is a general picture, yet it serves to link the thronging of the multitudes, which is so much insisted on by St. Mark, with the selection of an inner circle of disciples.

vii. It is characteristic of Mark to preserve visible links between incidents which elsewhere stand side by side. (Compare Matthew VI. iv.) Jesus goes into a house to eat bread, possibly for the purpose of meeting the deputation of scribes from Jerusalem. The pressure of the crowd disturbs the meal: this brings the brethren of Jesus to the rescue, and draws out the blasphemy of the scribes. At the end of Jesus's rebuke his brethren are still unable to get admittance through the crowd.

Page 121. *Is guilty of an eternal sin:* see above, note to *Matthew* VI. iv.

viii. The threefold division I have made of this section brings out its analogy with the corresponding section of Matthew (VII: see notes to that section). All the three evangelists make an epoch in Christ's ministry by this division between the outer multitude and the inner circle of disciples, and the addressing to each a different type of teaching. The first and third divisions of this section of *Mark* give examples of the public parables. There is the Parable of the Sower, which inaugurates this mode of teaching; the Parable of the Mustard Seed; and a third, peculiar to Mark, which suggests how the seed once planted must be left to work its own effects, the husbandman being unable to hurry its growth, or to interfere in any way until the harvest. Between 1 and 3 is the address to the inner circle of disciples, explaining the principle of the separation, and illustrating by the interpretation of the main parable. To this St. Mark adds teachings bringing out that these special instructions to the inner circle are only given them in order that they may pass them on to those outside. Here Mark introduces the image of the lamp—they are to be the light of the world—and the principle *With what measure ye mete*, etc., which Matthew embodies in the general discourse, or 'Sermon on the Mount.'

ix. The unity of this section is easily recognised: incidents on either side of the lake in the same journey to and fro.

xi. The connection of matter in this section seems to be as follows. The enlarged area of action made by the journeys of the apostles brings the fame of the new movement to the ears of Herod: the mention of this name leads to the story of the execution of John the Baptist. The return of the apostles is made an occasion for seeking rest: but the thronging of the multitudes into the desert prevents this, and leads to the miracle of feeding. Then Jesus seeks rest by night, and on his return to the disciples occurs the miracle on the sea. On his arrival on the other side there is fresh pressure of the multitude, and so we pass to xii. In *St. Matthew* (VIII. ii) it is the news of the Baptist's death, brought home by the apostles on their return that is made the motive for seeking rest.

Page 130. *Wheresoever ye enter into a house,* etc. We have here the substance rather than the full text of the commission. Compare above, note to *Matthew* V.

Page 134. *The Tradition of the Elders:* see above, note to *Matthew* VIII. iii.

Page 134, footnote. I have here, as elsewhere, used the modern form of a footnote to convey a parenthesis: the absence of this device from ancient MSS. gives often an appearance of awkwardness to style where there is none. (Compare page 175 of the *Ecclesiastes* volume.)

xiii. For the incident itself compare above, page 253.

xiv, xvi. Both sections illustrate Mark's power of vivid details.

Page 139. *And he charged them that they should tell no man of him* — page 142. *And he would not that any man should know it.* — Jesus seems to be unwilling that the recognition of the Messiahship shall stand alone, without the recognition of the Messiah's sufferings. It is part of his wider purpose to restrain the appeal to mere wonder working. Compare above, note to *Matthew* IV. i.

xviii. A comparison of this section with *Matthew* IX. ii is interesting. Matthew presents a series of important teachings,

Notes

the link between which is the idea of 'offences,' the whole arising out of an incident he preserves in which Jesus paid tribute to avoid giving offence. Mark, who omits that circumstance, interrupts the series of discourses by another incident, that of the man casting out devils in Christ's name but not following Christ. Possibly the series of teachings may have been linked together by the object lesson of a little child in the midst: Mark has preserved this visible link, Matthew the logical connection.

Page 143. *For every one shall be salted with fire . . . have salt in yourselves, and be at peace one with another.*—Compare *Matthew* III. ii: *Ye are the salt of the earth.* The connection of thought is not difficult: Ye are the purifying force of the world: this purifying force must be maintained at all costs, even at the cost of the purifying fire of suffering [viz. the sacrifices of which he has just spoken]: thus he bids them cast off for this purpose even their natural ambition and rivalry [*be at peace one with another*]. Fire is appropriately used for the supreme purifying power: compare *Matthew*, page 14, where it is contrasted with the weaker purifying power of water. John baptizes with water, but his mightier successor with fire.

Page 146. *But many that are first shall be last*, etc. The connection of this with what precedes is best seen in the fuller report of *Matthew:* see note to IX. iii.

xxv. For the Incident of the Fig tree compare note to *Matthew* X. i.

Page 154. *And the scribe said unto him, Of a truth, Master, thou hast well said*, etc. The difference of the two incidents as related here and in *St. Matthew* (page 83) is characteristic of the two writers. Mark gives the visible picture of a particular incident seen by an eye witness; Matthew is collecting a series of questions solved by Jesus, and the difference in personal character between this scribe and the other questioners does not concern him.

xxix. See note to *Matthew* XI.

xxx. See note to *Matthew* XII. i.

Page 161. *This is my blood of the covenant*, etc.: see below, note to page 188.

Page 163. *And a certain young man followed with him*, etc. Probably the explanation of this otherwise isolated circumstance is that it is one of the graphic details of which this gospel is full. A sleeper roused in the night follows to see what the disturbance is: the rough soldiers lay hold of his extemporised garment, and he flees naked. Another example of the mixture of curiosity and panic which was manifested by Peter on that night.

Appendix. Both the external evidence of MSS. and ancient authorities, and the internal evidence from the sentences themselves, concur in suggesting that this is not the final section of the gospel, but an appendix added subsequently because the conclusion (**xxxvi**) was abrupt. In style it appears, not a narrative, but a compendium of the appearances of Jesus after his resurrection: one of these appearances being the very incident which was related in the previous section.

Syllabus and Notes

to

The Epistles

AN EPISTLE TO HEBREWS

Syllabus

⁎₊⁎ A paragraph in the Syllabus usually represents a paragraph in the text.

[The epistle describes itself at its close as a 'word of exhortation.' Two lines of thought are traceable in it: (1) a strain of exhortation (indented in the syllabus to the left); and (2) distinct arguments approaching to digressions which establish particular points occurring in the general strain of exhortation (indented to the right). These digressive arguments include the most important parts of the epistle; the thoughts they contribute are gathered up by the strain of exhortation as it resumes.]

I

Now that God's scattered revelations to the fathers by prophets have become a full revelation through a Son, exalted after his finished work of purification as far above the angels as he is beyond them by inheritance:

> for the Scriptures speak not of the angels as 'sons'—they are 'winds,' 'flames of fire'—their mission is to do service for the sake of the heirs of salvation:

how much more earnest heed should we give not to drift away from this greater salvation — a salvation by one to whom 'all things' are subjected.

But not yet: Jesus hath been made 'a little lower than the angels' and exalted through death and sufferings, that the author of salvation might partake in all things pertaining to his brethren, and so be a merciful and faithful HIGH PRIEST between God and a sinful people.

II

Wherefore consider this High Priest of our confession — faithful as Moses, yet with more glory in proportion as a son is above a servant. Take heed that the evil heart of unbelief which kept the followers of Moses from 'entering into His rest' keep not us from the true 'rest.'

For it was the followers of Moses who provoked and were excluded, but it is to us that the psalmist's word of 'rest' must apply: not to the rest after the creation, nor the rest of the promised land: there must remain a Sabbath rest for God's people, a rest from works.

Let us hold fast our confession, confiding in a High Priest, tempted and thus able to succour the tempted, appointed like other priests by God, by obedience and suffering made perfect, and thus author of an eternal salvation, A HIGH PRIEST AFTER THE ORDER OF MELCHIZEDEK.

But is it any use to treat of this theme with those who linger in the milk of first principles instead of pressing on to strong meat and fulness of growth? Those who have lost the taste for the heavenly word have no means of renewing themselves, while they thus crucify afresh the Son of God. But your former love and diligence is earnest that you will press on to the fulness of hope, secured by God's promise and oath: a hope extending whither there has preceded us this High Priest for ever after the order of Melchizedek.

(1) Melchizedek ABIDETH A PRIEST CONTINUALLY. Abraham (and in Abraham the Levitical priesthood) paying to him tithes foreshadowed imperfections and change of Levitical law.—Jesus is surety of a better covenant: appointed by oath that can not be repented of; not mortal and therefore needing successors; not sinful and so needing daily sacrifices: by sacrifice of himself once for all perfected for evermore.

(2) Especially to be emphasised: our High Priest is minister of the TRUE TABERNACLE, of which the tabernacle made by Moses was but a shadow, and so is minister of a better covenant [founded on better promises]. Under the ordinances of the first covenant the High Priest passed with blood once a year through the first tabernacle into the Holy of Holies, the way to the holy place not yet having been made manifest: but Christ, through the more perfect tabernacle 'not made with hands' passed once for all with his own blood into the holy place, making eternal redemption.

(3) His better sacrifice makes him MEDIATOR OF A NEW

COVENANT: his death is the dedicatory death of the covenant — his blood is the cleansing for heavenly things, as the blood of bulls and goats was for their copies. — As death comes but once, and then is the judgment, so Christ's death is once for all, and then cometh his salvation. — The old sacrifices by their not ceasing to be offered confessed their imperfection: in Christ is realised the psalmist's vision that takes away 'sacrifices' and establishes a 'coming to do God's will' — here is the 'remission of sins' that accompanied the prophet's 'new covenant.'

III

With this High Priest then, and this way he has dedicated for us into the holy place, and with hearts thus sprinkled from an evil conscience, let us hold fast our confession and hope, that it waver not as the day approaches. — To shrink back after receiving knowledge of the truth will bring sorer doom than the violation of Moses' law. — Your former endurance needs to be supplemented by patience: it is 'BY FAITH that the righteous shall live.'

This 'faith' gives substance to future hopes, and dares to put the unseen to the test. — The glorious array of the fathers had witness borne to them that they thus made trial by faith, and yet received not, waiting for us before they could be made perfect.

Therefore with all these accepted witnesses to faith let us gird ourselves to our race, with eyes on our faith's captain. — Endure what is but chastening, that shall bring forth fruits of righteousness. — Strengthen one another — see also that no single poisonous root trouble the many.

Not to the material terrors of Moses' mount have ye come, but to the spiritual glories of Mount Zion and the mediator of the New Covenant: a voice then shook the earth, our promise is the 'Yet once more' of shaking that brings a kingdom not to be shaken.

IV

General exhortations. — Especially against being swayed by diverse doctrines: they of the tabernacle are no authorities for us, who go with Jesus outside the camp and share his reproach.

Notes

Page 175. *If the word spoken through angels proved stedfast* etc. The connection of angelic mediation with the giving of the law is hinted at in *Deuteronomy*, chapter xxxiii. 2; but was a widespread idea in New Testament times. Compare *Acts*, chapter vii. 35; *Galatians*, chapter iii. 19.

Page 176: quotations. The first quotation is from *Psalms* xxii. 22: the writer evidently reads it as a Messianic psalm. The other two are probably representations of *Isaiah*, chapter viii. 17, 18. The point of the citation is difficult to catch: it appears to be that Isaiah, accepting (in the words, *I will put my trust*, etc.) his function of being a 'sign' to Israel, associates with him in this function his own children (the *sharers in flesh* *and blood* of the next sentence). So the Son associates himself with flesh and blood in his work of mediation.

Page 177. *As was Moses in all His house:* compare *Numbers*, chapter xii. 7: *My servant Moses is not so; he is faithful in all mine house.*

Page 182. *As touching those who were once enlightened... it is impossible to renew them ... the while they crucify,* etc. This description of a spiritual state, hopeless as long as it lasts, may be compared with similar passages of the gospels: compare note on *Matthew* VI. iv.

Page 184. *Not after the law of a carnal commandment:* the context shows that *carnal* is used in the sense of limited by mortality. So page 187, *carnal ordinances.*

Page 186: footnote. Here as elsewhere I use the modern device of footnotes to convey parentheses which, as they stand in the text, obscure the argument, and give an impression of awkwardness of style, where there is in reality only difference of page setting.

Page 187. *Through the greater and more perfect tabernacle not made with hands.* Though the text does not explicitly state what point, in the elaborate analogy, is to be understood as antitype to 'tabernacle,' yet the words '*not made with hands*' call up the prominent saying of Christ: *Destroy this temple ... and in three days I will raise it up — he spake of the temple of his body.* (*John*, chapter ii. 19.)

Page 188. *For where a covenant is, there must of necessity be the death of him that made it. For a covenant is of force where there hath been death.* The text of the R.V. in these two

Notes — Hebrews

sentences changes the rendering of the word that runs through the whole passage from *covenant* to *testament*. As the margin says, the Greek word means both. But the argument requires that the same word be used throughout. Moreover the word *testament* in this connection introduces an image familiar to the English reader, but of no force to Hebrews, with whom 'testaments' in the sense of 'wills' were scarcely known. On the other hand, the image required by the whole context is one unfamiliar to the English reader, but perfectly intelligible to those to whom the epistle is addressed. The reference is to the sacrifices of animals which were the formal sign of a covenant between parties: the stroke of death being the irrevocable seal set on an agreement from which there can be no departing. An elaborate act of this kind accompanies the establishment of the covenant in *Exodus* (chapter xxiv): which indeed is kept in view throughout the whole of the remaining argument. — The same notion underlies the words of Christ in the Last Supper: *This cup is the new covenant in my blood* (*I Corinthians*, chapter xi. 25; the briefer form is given in *St. Matthew: this is my blood of the covenant*).

Page 192. *But my righteous one shall live by faith: and if he shrink back*, etc. The citation is from *Habakkuk*, chapter ii: but from the Greek version, which has a different sense and reference from the Hebrew version represented in our O.T.

Page 196. *Compassed about with so great a cloud of witnesses*. There is an ambiguity in the English word *witness* which does not hold of the original. The *cloud* is, not of spectators, but of those who *have had witness borne to them* that they were faithful: so throughout the preceding paragraphs.—*The sin which is admired of many:* the beautiful phrase of the R.V. and A.V. text: 'sin that doth so easily beset us' is hardly borne out by the Greek. The image is that of keeping on a fine garment though it hinders the running.

Page 198. *The blood of sprinkling that speaketh better than Abel:* a reference to *Genesis,* chapter iv. 10: *The voice of thy brother's blood crieth unto me from the ground.* So above: *He being dead yet speaketh* (page 193).

ST. JAMES

This is a miscellany of Wisdom literature: another 'Wisdom Epistle,' but of the simplest kind, is found in the *Book of Proverbs* (page 103 of that volume). In Wisdom literature it is natural to look for separate sayings, not a continuous argument. The forms followed by St. James are chiefly two: (1) The Maxim: a gnomic text, with a prose expansion. (The texts in this edition are printed in italics.) Compare above, page 248. Several of these maxims of this epistle may be termed 'Paradoxes.'—(2) The Essay. For both compare Introduction to the *Ecclesiasticus* volume, pages *xi–xiii.*—Of course the matter of the epistle is a Christianised form of traditional wisdom; and, as an outward mark, *my brethren* takes the place of the old formula, *my son.*

iv. This is the most elaborate and difficult of the essays of St. James. Its topic is the Sources of the Evil and Good in us. The opening note is temptation, or the struggle of evil and good. Then the origin of the Evil in us is put under the image of childbirth: one parent is the individual himself [or his will, we may say by analogy with the other paragraph], the other his lust: this is not a marriage but a seduction. The thought is carried forward to a second generation: lust, sin, death. — Passing to the origin of Good, the writer again uses the image of birth: the Divine will and the word of truth beget in us an *inborn word.* Development of good consists in listening for this inborn word (*swift to hear*), avoiding all that drowns the sound. Especially essential is the acting on this inborn word so far as heard: here the imagery changes to that of a mirror. Practical examples conclude the essay.

v. *If ye fulfil the royal law ... ye do well: but if ye have respect of persons ye commit sin.* The argument appears to be as follows: You take your stand on the letter of the law, 'Thou shalt love,' etc. and refuse to transgress it. But respecting persons is equally a transgression of the law: and to transgress in one point is as bad as to transgress in another. Rather, take your stand on Christian liberty and mercy.

vii. This essay is full of reminiscences of *Ecclesiasticus:* compare in that volume I. xxi, lix, lxxx; II. xviii.

ix. *But he giveth more grace.* The connection is obscure: perhaps it may be put thus. The spirit of longing envy in you is not of God's planting; but he will give more grace to overcome it in proportion to its strength (compare the suggestion of strength in the expression *long unto envying*): yet only to the humble. Wherefore, etc.

x. *He that speaketh against a brother ... speaketh against the law.* It is a characteristic of the epistle that it represents

Christian liberty, not as a relaxation of law, but as a higher law. He who censoriously interferes with his brother's freedom of action is attacking this supreme law of liberty.

EPISTLES OF ST. PETER: No. 1

Syllabus

₊ *A paragraph in the Syllabus usually represents a paragraph of the text.*

1

The epistle starts with a recital of the LIVING HOPE, restored through the resurrection of Jesus to the faithful, while they are being guarded to their final salvation: a theme of joy amid their manifold temptations, an object of search to the ancient prophets, an object of interest to angels.

The true attitude in presence of such a Hope: sober effort — holiness in place of former lusts — fear, alike in regard of the righteous Judge and the price of their redemption — fervent love of the brethren, lower love being purged away by obedience. — As babes born of the incorruptible seed of God's word to grow with spiritual milk unto salvation — as living stones to build up a spiritual house: a priesthood for spiritual sacrifices, an elect race, God's own possession.

2

More particular exhortations to the realisation of this attitude. First of all, by abstinence from fleshly lusts to become a testimony to the Gentiles — to silence outsiders by well-doing in all social relationships — as subjects — as servants (patient even to the froward, since Christ their redeemer was thus patient) — as wives (seeking the inner adornment of a quiet spirit) — as husbands.

To sum up: tenderly united among themselves to meet outside persecution, not by reviling back, but by blessing with the blessings of which they are heirs. — To suffer for well-doing is their calling, as Christ suffered for others' sins. — As Christ was put to death in the flesh [but quickened in the spirit, so as to preach to the disobedient spirits in prison] so let their own sufferings be made a death to the life of lust and a living to the will of God.

3

The end is at hand: let their sobriety, their love, their work, be all quickened. — The fiery trial must not be thought a strange thing by the partakers of Christ's sufferings: it means that judgment is beginning at the house of God. — Let the elder in his oversight and the younger in their subjection humble themselves under the mighty hand of God, waiting for their exaltation in due time.

Notes

Page 219. *Having been begotten again not of corruptible seed*, etc. While retaining the words of the R.V. I have altered the punctuation, so as to take this participial clause with what follows and not with what precedes. [The Greek admits of this.] There is little point in associating the idea of the incorruptible seed, so strongly emphasised, with the fervent love of the brethren. On the other hand, much strength is added to the passage if this incorruptible seed is made the first item in the continued image of *babes — spiritual milk . . . grow unto salvation*. This participial clause having been interrupted by a parenthesis, including a lengthy quotation, is linked on to another participial clause by a *therefore*, which repeats the causal relation implied in a participial clause. There is a similar use of *then* after the long parenthesis on page 224: *forasmuch then as Christ suffered in the flesh*.

Page 223. *For, He that would love life*, etc. The relevancy of the quotation is to the whole command (to meet persecution with blessing), not to the sentence immediately preceding.

Page 224. *For unto this end was the gospel preached even to the dead:* the *dead* are *the spirits in prison* of page 223: the position of the sentence shows that both the elements here asserted of Christ — put to death in the flesh, and ministering in the spirit to the dead — are pressed into the analogy between Christ and his followers: see Syllabus.

EPISTLES OF ST. PETER: No. II

Syllabus

✶ *A paragraph of the Syllabus usually represents a paragraph of the text.*

The epistle starts from the formula of greeting: Grace be multiplied to the possessors of the promises: a succession of graces, richly supplying an entrance into the eternal kingdom of Jesus Christ.

The life work of the writer is thus to stir up to remembrance of the coming of Christ — since he has been one of the eye witnesses of his majesty — and thus has a confirmation of the word of prophecy. — But just as there were false prophets of old, so now there shall be false teachers — moved by lasciviousness and covetousness — as to their certain doom, God's dealings with the angels, with Noah's world, with Sodom and Lot, are testimonies how God can deliver the godly and keep the unrighteous under punishment unto the day of judgment. — With every horror of defilement and disorder these re-ensnare to corruption those who are escaping: dogs returning to their own vomit.

This second epistle like the first is to stir up to remembrance of words received from prophets and from the Lord through apostles. Mockers will arise, casting doubts on Christ's coming because of the unbroken course of things since the creation — but as the old world by water so the present world shall perish by fire — with the Lord a day and a thousand years are alike: the judgment will come like a thief in the night. — Live in the light of this coming judgment, and account the longsuffering of the Lord as salvation.

THE EPISTLE OF ST. JUDE

Syllabus

⁎ *A paragraph of the Syllabus usually represents a paragraph of the text.*

The writer's general purpose to write quickened by the privy entering in of corrupters: his word is, contend for the faith once for all delivered to the saints.

Remember the judgment of the Israelites in the wilderness, of the fallen angels, of Sodom and Gomorrah — of like kind are these corrupters: fleshly and disorderly, things of horror — of these Enoch prophesied destruction — and the Lord Jesus Christ forewarned. — For yourselves: build up yourselves in your most holy faith — and on the erring have mercy, though mercy have to mingle with hate.

INDEX

AND

REFERENCE TABLE

REFERENCE TABLE

To connect the Numbering of the Present Edition with the Chapters and Verses of the Bible

ST. MATTHEW

		Chap.	Verse	Page
Genealogy.............................		I	1	5
I	The Birth of Jesus..................		18	9
		II	1	10
II	John the Baptist and the Appearance of Jesus in Public.................	III	1	13
		IV	1	14
III	Opening of the Ministry of Jesus and the Sevenfold Discourse...............		17	17
		V	1	18
	i......................................		3	18
	ii.....................................		13	19
	iii....................................		14	19
	iv.....................................		17	19
	v......................................	VI	1	22
	vi.....................................		19	24
	vii....................................	VII	1	26
IV	First Impressions: Gathering of Disciples and Hints of Antagonism			
	i......................................		28	29
		VIII	1	29
	ii.....................................		23	31

Reference Table

		Chap.	Verse	Page
	iii..	IX	1	32
	iv..		18	34
V	Organisation of Apostles and the Sevenfold Commission........................		35	36
		X	1	36
		XI	1	40
VI	Growing Isolation of Jesus and His Ministry			
	i...		2	41
	ii..		20	42
	iii...	XII	1	43
	iv...		22	45
VII	The Public Parable and the Private Interpretation...........................	XIII	1	49
	i...		3	49
	ii..		24	51
	iii...		31	52
	iv...		33	52
	v..		44	53
	vi...		45	53
	vii..		47	54
VIII	The Greater Miracles and the Growing Antagonism			
	i...		53	55
	ii..	XIV	1	55
	iii...	XV	1	58
	iv...		21	60
	v..		29	60
		XVI	1	61
IX	Fuller Recognition by the Disciples of the Kingdom and Questions arising thereupon			

Reference Table

		Chap.	Verse	Page
	i.................................	XVI	13	63
		XVII	1	64
	ii................................		22	66
		XVIII	1	67
	iii...............................	XIX	1	70
		XX	1	73
	iv...............................		17	74
X	Entry into Jerusalem and Final Breach with the Ruling Classes			
	i.................................	XXI	1	76
	ii................................		23	78
		XXII	1	80
	iii...............................		15	82
	iv...............................	XXIII	1	84
XI	Discourse to the Disciples: The Sevenfold Revelation of the End........	XXIV	1	88
		XXV	1	92
XII	The Passion and Resurrection of Jesus			
	i.................................	XXVI	1	96
	ii................................		17	97
	iii...............................		30	98
	iv...............................	XXVII	1	102
	v................................		27	104
	vi...............................		57	106
	vii..............................	XXVIII	1	107

ST. MARK

i	....	I	1	113
ii	....		14	114
iii	....		40	116

Reference Table

	Chap.	Verse	Page
	II	1	117
iv		13	118
v		23	119
	III	1	119
vi		7	120
vii		20	121
viii	IV	1	122
ix		35	125
	V	1	125
x	VI	1	129
xi		6	129
xii	VII	1	133
xiii		24	135
xiv		31	136
xv	VIII	1	136
xvi		22	138
xvii		27	139
	IX	1	140
xviii		30	142
xix	X	1	144
xx		13	145
xxi		17	145
xxii		32	146
xxiii		46	148
xxiv	XI	1	149
xxv		11	149
xxvi		27	151
	XII	1	151
xxvii		13	153
xxviii		41	155

Reference Table

	Chap.	Verse	Page
xxix	XIII	1	156
xxx	XIV	1	159
xxxi		12	160
xxxii		26	161
xxxiii	XV	1	165
xxxiv		16	166
xxxv		42	168
xxxvi	XVI	1	168
Appendix		9	169

HEBREWS

	Chap.	Verse	Page
I	I	1	173
	II	1	175
II	III	1	177
	IV	1	178
	V	1	180
	VI	1	181
	VII	1	183
	VIII	1	185
	IX	1	186
	X	1	189
III		19	191
	XI	1	192
	XII	1	196
IV	XIII	1	198

ST. JAMES

	Chap.	Verse	Page
Superscription	I	1	203
i The Joy of Temptation		2	203
ii The Prayer for Wisdom		5	203

Reference Table

		Chap.	Verse	Page
iii	A Paradox of High and Low	I	9	204
iv	On the Sources of the Evil and the Good in us		12	204
v	On Respect of Persons	II	1	206
vi	Faith and Works		14	207
vii	The Responsibility of Speech	III	1	208
viii	The Earthly Wisdom and the Wisdom from Above		13	209
ix	On Worldly Pleasures	IV	1	210
x	A Maxim against Judging		11	211
xi	The Judgment to Come		13	212
		V	1	212
xii	The Blessed Work of Converting		19	214

I ST. PETER

Superscription	I	1	217
1.		3	217
	II	1	219
2.		11	221
	III	1	222
	IV	1	224
3.		7	224
	V	1	225

II ST. PETER

Superscription	I	1	231
Epistle		2	231
	II	1	233
	III	1	235

Reference Table

ST. JUDE

	Verse	Page
Superscription	1	241
Epistle	3	241

Small 18mo. Cloth extra, 50 cents each; Leather, 60 cents.

The Modern Reader's Bible.

A Series of Books from the Sacred Scriptures,
presented in Modern Literary Form,

BY

RICHARD G. MOULTON,

M.A. (Camb.), Ph.D. (Penn.),

Professor of Literature in English in the University of Chicago.

PRESS COMMENTS.

The Outlook, New York. "The effect of these changes back to the original forms under which the sacred writings first appeared will be, for the vast majority of readers, a surprise and delight; they will feel as if they had come upon new spiritual and intellectual treasures, and they will appreciate for the first time how much the Bible has suffered from the hands of those who have treated it without reference to its literary quality. In view of the significance and possible results of Professor Moulton's undertaking, it is not too much to pronounce it one of the most important spiritual and literary events of the times. It is part of the renaissance of Biblical study; but it may mean, and in our judgment it does mean, the renewal of a fresh and deep impression of the beauty and power of the supreme spiritual writing of the world."

Presbyterian and Reformed Review. "Unquestionably here is a task worth carrying out: and it is to be said at once that Dr. Moulton has carried it out with great skill and helpfulness. Both the introduction and the notes are distinct contributions to the better understanding and higher appreciation of the literary character, features and beauties of the Biblical books treated."

THE MACMILLAN COMPANY
66 FIFTH AVENUE, NEW YORK

WISDOM SERIES

IN FOUR VOLUMES

THE PROVERBS
A Miscellany of Sayings and Poems embodying Isolated Observations of Life.

ECCLESIASTICUS
A Miscellany including longer compositions, still embodying only Isolated Observations of Life.

ECCLESIASTES — WISDOM OF SOLOMON
Each is a Series of Connected Writings embodying, from different standpoints, a Solution of the Whole Mystery of Life.

THE BOOK OF JOB
A Dramatic Poem in which are embodied Varying Solutions of the Mystery of Life.

DEUTERONOMY
The Orations and Songs of Moses, constituting his Farewell to the People of Israel.

BIBLICAL IDYLS
The Lyric Idyl of Solomon's Song, and the Epic Idyls of Ruth, Esther, and Tobit.

THE PSALMS (Two Volumes)
Containing the whole of The Psalms and also the Book of Lamentations.

SELECT MASTERPIECES OF BIBLICAL LITERATURE

HISTORY SERIES
IN FIVE VOLUMES

GENESIS
Bible History, Part I : Formation of the Chosen Nation.

THE EXODUS
Bible History, Part II: Migration of the Chosen Nation to the Land of Promise. — Book of Exodus, with Leviticus and Numbers.

THE JUDGES
Bible History, Part III: The Chosen Nation in its Efforts towards Secular Government. — Books of Joshua, Judges, I Samuel.

THE KINGS
Bible History, Part IV: The Chosen Nation under a Secular Government side by side with a Theocracy. — Books of II Samuel, I and II Kings.

THE CHRONICLES
Ecclesiastical History of the Chosen Nation. — Books of Chronicles, Ezra, Nehemiah.

PROPHECY SERIES
IN FOUR VOLUMES

ISAIAH
The vision of Isaiah, the Son of Amoz, which he saw concerning Judah and Jerusalem in the days of Uzziah, Jotham, Ahaz, and Hezekiah, Kings of Judah.

EZEKIEL
The prophetic works of Ezekiel.

JEREMIAH
The words of Jeremiah, the Son of Hilkiah, to whom the Word of the Lord came in the days of Josiah, Jehoiakim, and Zedekiah, Kings of Judah.

DANIEL AND THE MINOR PROPHETS

Containing The Book of Daniel, The Prophecy of Hosea, The Prophecy of Joel, The Book of Amos, The Vision of Obadiah, The Book of Jonah, The Prophecy of Micah, The Oracle Concerning Nineveh and the Book of Nahum, The Oracle which Habakkuk did see, The Prophecy of Zephaniah, The Book of Haggai, The Book of Zechariah, and other anonymous prophecies.

NEW TESTAMENT SERIES

IN FOUR VOLUMES

ST. MATTHEW, ST. MARK, and the GENERAL EPISTLES

Containing The Gospel according to St. Matthew, The Gospel according to St. Mark, an Epistle to the Hebrews, The Epistle of St. James, The Epistles of St. Peter, and The Epistle of St. Jude.

ST. LUKE and ST. PAUL (Two Volumes)

Containing The Gospel of St. Luke, The Acts of the Apostles, with the Pauline Epistles introduced at the several points of the history to which they are usually referred. An opportunity will thus be afforded of studying, without the interruption of comment or discussion, the continuous History of the New Testament Church as presented by itself.

ST. JOHN

Containing the Gospel, Epistles, and Revelation of St. John.

THE MACMILLAN COMPANY
66 FIFTH AVENUE, NEW YORK

www.ingramcontent.com/pod-product-compliance
Lightning Source LLC
Chambersburg PA
CBHW021157230426
43667CB00006B/443